Christmas Treats

STEP-BY-STEP
Christmas Treats

Janice Murfitt

Photography by Edward Allwright

ACROPOLIS
BOOKS

First published in 1994 by Lorenz Books

© Anness Publishing Limited

Lorenz Books is an imprint of
Anness Publishing Limited
Boundary Row Studios
1 Boundary Row
London SE1 8HP

ISBN 1 85967 004 0

Distributed in Australia by Treasure Press

This edition exclusively published
in South-east Asia by
Richard Blady Publishing
17 Madeley Road, Ealing
London W5 2LA

A CIP catalogue record is available from the British Library.

Editorial Director: Joanna Lorenz
Series Editor: Lindsay Porter
Designer: Peter Laws
Jacket Designer: Peter Butler
Photographer: Edward Allwright
Stylist: Maria Kelly

MEASUREMENTS
Three sets of equivalent measurements have been provided in the recipes here, in the following
order: Metric, Imperial and American. It is essential that units of measurement are not mixed
within each recipe. Where conversions result in awkward numbers, these have been rounded for
convenience, but are accurate enough to produce successful results.

Printed and bound by Graphicom S.r.l., Vincenza

CONTENTS

INTRODUCTION

Christmas is such a wonderful time, a time full of excitement and surprises. Every city, town and village enters into the spirit, decorating the streets with brightly coloured lights and festive trees, and filling the air with the sound of Christmas carols. Shops are overflowing with Christmas fare, tempting treats and gifts, and there is certainly a magical feeling everywhere.

There is always so much to plan at Christmastime – and organizing and choosing Christmas presents must be near the top of the list. This book is packed full of tempting festive treats that you can make yourself, from sweets, candies, individual puddings and cakes, to savoury butters, pâtés and spiced vinegars. We'll show you how to present your treasures in pretty wrapping paper and boxes, to make delightful, delicious presents with a personal touch.

Share the true spirit of Christmas by making your own gifts for friends and family, and make *Step-by-Step Christmas Treats* part of the celebrations.

Equipment

Some of the recipes that follow call for specialized items of equipment to obtain the best results. These are readily available from standard kitchenware suppliers. Look after your equipment well and it should never need replacing. Always ensure that metal cutters, tins and utensils are kept in a warm dry place to prevent any discoloration and store piping nozzles in rigid containers to prevent them from being damaged.

Baking sheets
Good quality steel sheets in different sizes and without sides are best as these will not buckle during cooking.

Chopping boards
These are for chopping or rolling out pastry or icing, and can be made of wood or acrylic. Acrylic is non-stick and especially good for working with marzipan, icing and sugar.

Cooling racks
Wide and narrow mesh racks in a variety of sizes are needed for drying and cooling cakes, icing, chocolate and glacé fruits.

Cutters
A set of round, oval, square, plain or fluted cutters is necessary for cutting out biscuits, pastry or icing shapes.

Flour and sugar dredgers
These are used for lightly dusting surfaces with flour before rolling out doughs and for dredging sugar on top of cakes and pastries.

Flower and leaf cutters
Tiny metal cutters are available in almost any shape or size to match any flower bloom or leaf shape.

Flower mat
This mat is invaluable for giving sugar flowers and leaves a natural shape while working the paste; foam sponge may be used as a substitute.

Food mixers and processors
Large food mixers are good for mixing large cake quantities quickly and thoroughly. They are ideal for chopping and crushing or for making pastry or bread doughs and will cut down on preparation time.

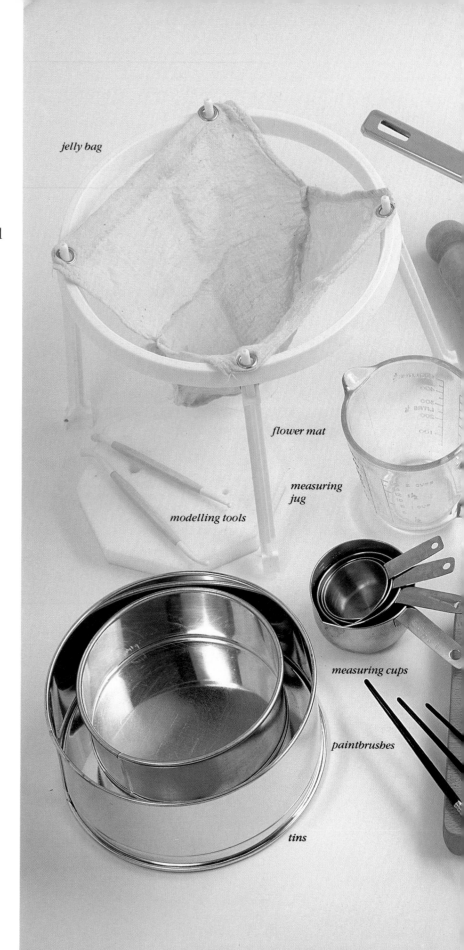

jelly bag

flower mat

measuring jug

modelling tools

measuring cups

paintbrushes

tins

saucepan

preserving jar

tins

measuring spoons

cooling rack

baking sheet

jam funnel

grater

flour dredger

rolling pin

potato peeler

knives

flower and leaf cutters

sieve

glazing brush

palette knives

cutters

mixing bowls

chopping board

Glazing brushes
Keep a variety of sizes for glazing cakes, brushing pastry and greasing tins. They are available in small, medium and large sizes.

Graters
A 4- or 6-sided grater with a variety of grating sizes is necessary for many ingredients.

Jam funnels
These are made of plastic or stainless steel and are invaluable for filling jars with jam, jelly or chutney without spillage or drips. Use narrow funnels for filling bottles.

Jelly bag
A good quality jelly bag with a very fine weave will ensure that the jelly is crystal clear. A stand is useful but you can improvise with an upturned stool or hook.

Knives
Good quality knives are an investment. Choose a long-bladed knife for slicing, a medium one for chopping and a small knife for paring.

Measuring cups
These are useful for measuring dry ingredients in American cup sizes.

Measuring jugs
These can be large or small, heatproof or plastic, for accurate measuring of liquids.

Measuring spoons
These are ideal for the consistent measuring of spoon sizes as general spoons vary widely.

Mixing bowls
Keep several different sizes including heatproof bowls, for whisked mixtures and sugar syrup. The insides should have a smooth rounded finish to ensure thorough mixing.

Modelling tools
These are a good investment if you enjoy cake decoration or modelling. The bone tool is needed for making flowers and the scalpel for cutting out shapes. The scribing tool is invaluable for piercing, marking out and outlining.

Muslin
Very fine cotton muslin is invaluable for straining mixtures in place of a jelly bag, for enclosing pickling spices for flavouring or infusing, and for covering icing to keep it from drying.

Nozzles
Straight-sided, good quality metal piping nozzles will give a good clean result. They are expensive but should not need replacing if treated with care.

Paintbrushes
A wide selection is available from good cake icing and decorating suppliers. Use paintbrushes for painting on food colourings, sticking sugar pieces together with Gum Glaze and for dusting with food colouring dusts.

Palette
This is useful for keeping small quantities of food colouring dusts separate.

Palette knives
These are essential for all types of cooking especially

small, crank-handled knives for fine icing and sugar work. They are available with small, medium and large blades.

Pencil, rubber and scissors
These are always necessary for drawing around tin sizes on paper, measuring tin sizes and for cutting out paper templates.

Potato peeler
Use to pare rinds from fruit, or chocolate curls off blocks of chocolate.

Rolling pins
Smooth, straight-ended rolling pins made of wood or acrylic are useful for pastry, dough and icing. Acrylic non-stick rolling pins come in several sizes.

Sieves
Small and fine mesh sieves made of wire or nylon are useful for sieving and straining ingredients and mixtures.

Tins
Round, square or Swiss roll cake tins and moulds should be of the best quality. Good quality metal tins will not bend or warp during cooking and should never need replacing if they are well looked after.

Apricot Glaze

It is always a good idea to make a large quantity of apricot glaze, especially if you need it for a celebration cake.

Makes 450 g/1 lb/2 cups

INGREDIENTS
450 g/1 lb/2 cups apricot jam
30 ml/2 tbsp water

1 Place the jam and water into a saucepan, and heat gently, stirring occasionally until melted.

2 Boil the jam rapidly for 1 minute, then strain through a sieve. Rub through as much fruit as possible, using a spoon, and discard any skins left in the sieve.

3 Pour the glaze into a clean, hot jar, seal with a clean lid and cool. Store in the fridge where it will keep well for up to 2 months.

Royal Icing

Royal icing will dry very hard. It is ideal for covering cakes and piping decorations.

Makes 450 g/1 lb/2 cups

INGREDIENTS
2 × size 3 egg whites
¼ tsp lemon juice
450 g/1 lb/2 cups icing sugar, sieved
5 ml/1 tsp glycerine

1 Place the egg whites and lemon juice into a clean bowl. Stir, using a clean wooden spoon to break up the whites.

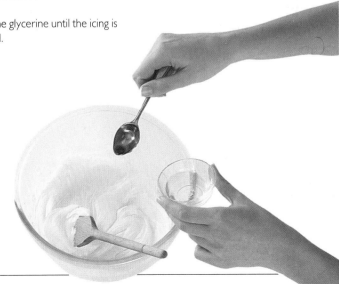

2 Add a little of the icing sugar and mix well until the mixture is the consistency of unwhipped cream. Continue to add small quantities of icing sugar until the desired consistency has been reached, mixing well between each addition.

3 Stir in the glycerine until the icing is well blended.

Lining a Deep Cake Tin of any Shape

For rich or light fruit cakes, use good quality fixed-base deep cake tins. Ensure that you have the correct size of tin for the quantity of cake mixture.

1 Place the tin on a piece of double thickness greaseproof paper or non-stick baking paper and draw around the base following the tin shape. Cut out the marked shape with a pair of scissors.

2 Measure and cut a strip of double thickness greaseproof paper or non-stick baking paper long enough to wrap around the outside of the tin with a small overlap and to stand 2.5 cm/1 in above the top of the tin.

3 Brush the base and sides of the tin with melted white fat or oil. Place the cut-out paper shape in the base of the tin and press flat. Fit the double strip of greaseproof paper or non-stick baking paper inside the tin, pressing well against the sides and making sharp creases where the paper fits into the corners of the tin. Ensure that the paper strip is level and fits neatly without any creases. Brush the base and sides well with melted white fat or oil.

4 Measure and fit a double thickness strip of brown paper around the outside of the tin. Tie securely with string.

5 Line a baking sheet with several layers of brown paper and stand your prepared cake tin in the centre.

Templates

For gingerbread houses, you may find it easier to use a template for the walls and roof of the house.

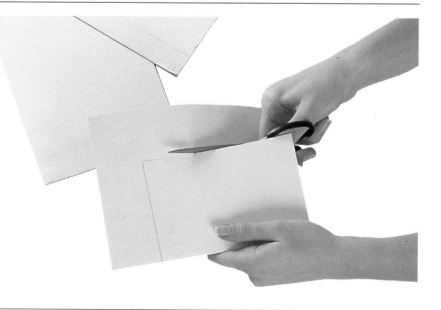

1 Draw the dimensions required onto stiff card, and cut out. Position on top of the rolled out dough, and cut around the card shape with a pair of scissors or sharp knife.

Preparing Containers for Preserves

It is most important that the containers used to hold preserves have no cracks or chips which could harbour micro-organisms and turn the preserve bad. Ideally, all lids, stoppers and corks should be new, but if you are using old ones ensure they are in good condition without any corrosion, perished rubber seals, or ill-fitting stoppers.

1 To Clean Jars and Bottles: wash them in plenty of hot soapy water using a bottle brush to get into the crevices at the base and around the neck of the container. Rinse well in clean water and dry thoroughly. Do the same for the lids and stoppers. Alternatively use a dishwasher.

2 To Sterilize: a solution of Campden sterilizing tablets and water is best for bottles and corks. Make up and use the solution following the directions on the packet.

3 Pour the solution into the containers through a funnel, leave for the amount of time specified on the packet, then pour out. Refrigerated syrups, cordials and juices will keep for 4 weeks, but sterilizing with a Campden solution will extend their storage to 1 year.

Melting Chocolate

Working with chocolate can be tricky but these instructions are guaranteed fool-proof.

1 Always use fresh chocolate to ensure a good result. Break the chocolate into small pieces and place in a large, dry, clean bowl over a saucepan of hand-hot water.

2 Ensure that the base of the bowl does not touch the water and there are no spaces between the bowl and the rim of the saucepan which might cause steam and condensation to get into the chocolate, rendering it thick and unusable.

3 Do not beat the chocolate, but stir occasionally while it is melting. Don't try to hurry the process: the chocolate temperature should never exceed 38–43°C/100–110°F, otherwise when it eventually sets, the surface will be dull and covered in streaks.

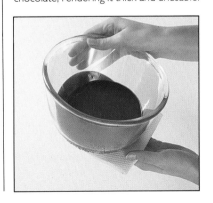

4 Leave the bowl over hand-hot water during use, unless you want the chocolate to become thicker. Wipe the base of the bowl to remove any condensation.

Sweet Ingredients

Almonds
Almonds may be used blanched or with the skin intact. Blanched almonds, with the skins removed, have a sweet flavour and are ideal for cakes. Almonds with the skin intact are ideal for sweets, and delicious coated in chocolate or caramel.

Angelica
Green angelica stems preserved in sugar are used for cake decorating.

Chocolate
Chocolate in all its many forms is a firm favourite at Christmastime. Milk chocolate has a softer texture and sweeter flavour than plain chocolate. Plain chocolate, with its strong, rich flavour is ideal for melting and cooking. White chocolate is a product made with cocoa butter, which imparts a sweet, delicate flavour without the strong cocoa taste.

milk chocolate

plain chocolate

Cinnamon
Cinnamon may be used ground, or as a whole 'stick'. Cinnamon sticks impart a wonderful flavour to oils, vinegars and drinks.

Cloves
Cloves are full of flavour and are a delicious addition to spiced vinegars.

Crystallized ginger
This is preserved ginger root, coated in sugar. Its pungent flavour and crunchy outer layer makes it a good addition to home-made chocolates and sweets.

Dates
Fresh or dried, dates are used in cakes, sweets, home-made chocolates and preserves.

Dried fruit
Mixed dried fruit is a blend of raisins, sultanas, currants, mixed peel and cherries, essential for Christmas cakes and puddings. Dried fruits are very nutritious, and have a very concentrated flavour.

Glacé fruit
Almost any fruit may be preserved in sugar syrup, and the colourful results make beautiful decorations. These can be fairly expensive to buy, but are very simple to make at home.

Hazelnuts
Hazelnuts may be used chopped in praline or cake mixtures, or finely ground.

Mace
Mace is the dried outer skin of the nutmeg, most often used ground. It has a milder flavour than nutmeg.

Nutmeg
Nutmeg can be bought whole, or as a powder. Freshly grated nutmeg has a wonderful flavour and aroma, and will impart a more powerful taste than the powdered form.

Pecan nuts
These nuts are similar to walnuts, but have a milder flavour. They make wonderful eating straight out of the shells, or may be bought as halves, or pieces for decoration and cooking.

Walnuts
Walnuts may be purchased in their shells, as walnut halves (ideal for decoration) or chopped for cake mixtures.

walnuts

almonds

blanched almonds

hazelnuts

mixed dried fruit

crystallized ginger

glacé fruit

pecan nuts

dried apricots

angelica

cloves

mace

dried figs

nutmeg

cinnamon

Fresh Fruit

peaches

apricots

apples

Apples
So many varieties are available at Christmastime, and all have their own characteristics – soft or crisp flesh, red, green or golden skins. Choose firm apples for glacé fruits.

Apricots
Choose firm, ripe apricots for the best colour and flavour.

Cherries
Purchase when in season, and use for glacé fruits or fruits in liqueurs. They are available at Christmastime, but are expensive.

Clementines
These are available most of the year and may be used for glacé fruits, preserves or flavouring brandy.

Cranberries
These jewel-bright fruits are a colourful Christmas addition, available fresh at Christmastime, or frozen.

Grapes
A lovely addition to a Christmas fruit bowl. Available red, green or black, with or without seeds.

Kumquats
These tiny orange fruits have a citrus flavour. They may be used for glacé fruits, or making liqueurs, with the skin intact.

Lemons
Buy small lemons with fine skins for the best juice.

Limes
Small limes with smooth, bright green skins have the best flavour.

Lychees
A Christmas treat; choose pink-skinned fruits with sweet white flesh.

Paw paws
An exotic fruit, increasingly available in good supermarkets. Paw paws have a sweet pink flesh. Discard the seeds and skin, and use for glacé fruits or fruits in liqueurs.

Peaches
Peaches are best purchased in the summer, when they are in peak condition. They may sometimes be available at Christmastime – but at a cost. Ensure they are not bruised or damaged when buying. Use for fruits in liqueurs.

Pears
Many varieties of pear are available. Make chutney when they are plentiful.

Physalis
Physalis or Cape gooseberries have a paper thin husk which should be peeled back before eating.

Plums
These are available all year round, but it is best to make use of indigenous varieties when in season.

Star fruit
These exotic fruits are available all the year round in good supermarkets. They are excellent preserved in liqueurs or used as glacé fruits.

Strawberries
Make the most of strawberries when in season, and bottle or use for preserves.

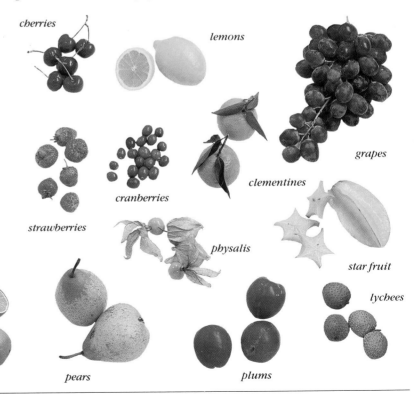

cherries

lemons

grapes

strawberries

cranberries

clementines

physalis

star fruit

lychees

limes

pears

plums

Savoury Ingredients

The following are just some of the ingredients used in the savoury recipes in this book. Always use the freshest, best quality ingredients available.

Anchovies
These have a very concentrated flavour, and are a great addition to fish pâtés.

Bacon slices
Back or streaky bacon keeps home-made pâtés moist and full of flavour.

Bay leaves
Bay leaves are available fresh or dried. They make a flavourful and decorative addition to bottled oils and vinegars.

Basil
A wonderfully aromatic herb used in oils and vinegars.

Celery
Celery imparts a great texture to vegetable chutneys and pickles.

Cheshire cheese
A mild cheese with a crumbly texture, use in potted spreads.

Chillies
Fresh chillies must be handled carefully. Remove the seeds from chillies to lessen their impact.

Dill
Dill is particularly suited to fish dishes. The leaf may be finely chopped and added to pâtés.

Garlic
Fresh bulbs of garlic divide into single cloves, which may be used crushed or whole.

Jarlsburg cheese
A Norwegian cheese similar to Emmenthal, good for cheese spreads.

Kippers
Kippers are smoked herrings; use in fish pâtés.

Olives
Olives, both black and green, impart a strong flavour and colour to pâtés and spreads.

Onions
Use large onions for chutneys and small onions pickled whole.

Parmesan cheese
A strongly flavoured cheese from Italy. Use freshly grated for the best flavour.

Peppers
Red, yellow and green peppers may be preserved in oil, or used in pepper jelly.

Peppercorns
Green and black peppercorns impart flavour and decoration to oils and vinegars. Pink peppercorns are so-called because of their appearance, but they are not true peppercorns.

Root ginger
Use the fresh root grated in sweet or savoury dishes.

Rosemary
Use rosemary sparingly in meat dishes, or add to oils and vinegars.

Sage
Sage is available throughout the year. Use in herbed vinegars and flavoured butters.

Salmon
Fresh salmon fillet may be used in pâtés and spreads.

Shropshire cheese
This red, blue-veined cheese is a good addition to cheese spreads.

Thyme
Thyme may be added to oils and vinegars, or peppers preserved in oil.

Tomatoes
Cherry tomatoes have the best flavour; larger tomatoes are good for cooking.

onions

basil

thyme

white peppercorns

pink peppercorns

green peppercorns

bay leaves

ginger

dill

anchovies

celery

olives

kipper

peppers

sage

bacon slices

smoked salmon

chillies

rosemary

Jarlsburg cheese

tomatoes

Parmesan cheese

garlic

Shropshire cheese

Cheshire cheese

PRESENTATION IDEAS

All of the recipes in this book have been devised to be given as gifts, although they are so delicious you are sure to want to keep a batch yourself. There are many ways of packaging your gifts; the following are just a few ideas.

Marzipan fruits

Marzipan fruits look so delightful it's a shame to hide them away.

1 Choose a transparent container to show the fruits to best effect. This one is very simple in design, but you may wish to choose a more elaborate, glass container. Carefully position the fruits inside the container.

2 Finish with a co-ordinating ribbon or decoration, secured to the lid with double-sided tape.

Christmas cakes

These little cakes make ideal gifts. Prettily packaged they are the very essence of Christmas.

1 For the container, a simple cardboard box covered in decorative paper was used. Line this with tissue paper in a festive colour.

2 Carefully place the cake in the box, and cover with the remaining tissue paper. Please note, this packaging is purely decorative, and will not protect the cake if you are planning to send it long distances or in the post.

Potted spreads and butters

Spreads and flavoured butters are enchanting packed in little jars. Sterilize the container as explained earlier, pack with the chosen spread and decorate as follows.

1 Decorate the top with ribbon curls in suitable colours (you may want to reflect the colours of the contents of the jars). Fix the ribbon curls in place with double-sided tape.

2 If you wish to present several assorted jars, pack them in a bag made of decorative wrapping paper.

Sweets and biscuits

If your gift will be given, and eaten, relatively quickly, and the contents do not need to be stored in an airtight container, then a pretty box lined with tissue paper may be the answer.

1 Line your chosen container with 3–4 sheets of co-ordinating tissue paper. After positioning the first piece, lay the others on top, alternating the corners to fill the spaces. Crumpled tissue paper has a charm all its own. You may wish to crumple it first, then lightly smooth out.

2 Carefully place the contents inside the box, and fold excess tissue over the top for extra security.

Gift Wrappings

The emphasis on attractive gift wrappings has increased considerably in recent years. It is relatively simple to make small gifts at home and package them beautifully. Personalized gifts are as much a joy to give as receive, and will mean so much more.

There are many shops that specialize in gift wrapping materials. Papers, ribbons, different types of boxes, containers, labels and cards are all available. When making your own Christmas gifts, look out for unusual accessories with which to enhance the packaging of the fruits of your labours.

Boxes
These make wonderful containers for chocolates, sweets, cakes or biscuits. You will find many different designs, colours and sizes in stationers, paper specialists or large stores.

Fabrics
Choose fabrics printed with Christmas designs to make a simple drawstring bag or stocking shape as a container for a small gift. Cover the tops of preserves with a circle of fabric over the cellophane discs and cover boxes with bright fabrics using a clear fabric adhesive. You can also add ribbons or cut-out shapes.

Gift bags
These are especially useful for packing awkwardly shaped gifts such as pots of preserves or bottles. They come in a variety of sizes and often have a matching gift label attached.

Gift cards and tags
These are often available to co-ordinate with your chosen paper, box or container. You can easily make your own tags by sticking your chosen paper onto a plain piece of card before making a hole in the corner and adding a ribbon.

Glass bottles
There is now an extensive range of recycled glass containers in all sizes, suitable for bottling drinks, flavoured oils and herbed vinegars. Many are available complete with their own air-tight stoppers or corks.

Glass jars
Assorted sizes of glass jars with screw-topped lids are invaluable for jams, jellies, savoury butters and spreads. Found mostly in kitchen departments or shops, some jars come in wonderful shapes and have corks to seal the tops.

Ribbons
The choice is overwhelming; even the simplest ribbons can transform a gift more than any other packaging.

Small dishes
The choice is quite daunting and is limited only by how much you are willing to pay. Choose from rustic pottery dishes which are fun to receive, or plain white china presented in brightly coloured wrapping paper. For a very special gift, choose a fine porcelain dish and place it in a box tied with co-ordinating ribbon.

Tins
These are often sold to store pens and pencils but make excellent air-tight containers for biscuits, sweets or small cakes, and can be found in many large stores, kitchen shops and stationers.

Right: *Bags and baskets, cards and tags, ribbons and wrappings of all kinds can be used to enhance your home-made gifts.*

Chocolate Boxes

These tiny chocolate boxes make the perfect containers for handmade chocolates or sweets. Use white or milk chocolate with dark trimmings to vary the theme.

Makes 4

INGREDIENTS
225 g/8 oz/8 squares plain, or milk
    chocolate, melted
50 g/2 oz/2 squares white chocolate

DECORATION
handmade chocolates or sweets, to fill
2 m/2 yd ribbon, 1 cm/½ in wide

milk chocolate

plain chocolate

white chocolate

2 Pour all but 1 tbsp of the chocolate over the baking paper and quickly spread to the edges using a palette knife. Pick up 2 corners of the paper and drop; do this several times on each side to level the surface of the chocolate.

1 Line a large baking sheet with non-stick baking paper. Remove the bowl of melted chocolate from the heat and wipe the condensation off the base of the bowl.

3 Leave the chocolate until almost set but still pliable. Place a clean piece of non-stick baking paper on the surface, invert the chocolate sheet and peel the paper away from the back of the chocolate. Using a ruler and a scalpel or sharp knife, measure and cut the chocolate sheet into 16 × 5 cm/2 in squares to form the sides of the boxes. Measure and cut out 8 × 5.5 cm/2¼ in squares for the lids and bases of each of the boxes.

4 To assemble the boxes, paint a little of the remaining melted chocolate along the top edges of a chocolate square using a fine brush. Place the side pieces in position one at a time, brushing the side edges to join the 4 squares together to form a box. Leave to set. Repeat to make the remaining 3 boxes.

5 Melt the white chocolate and spoon into a greaseproof paper piping bag. Fold down the top and snip off the point. Pipe 20 chocolate loops onto a sheet of baking paper and leave them to set.

6 Decorate the sides of the boxes with chocolate loops, each secured with a bead of white chocolate. Alternatively, wrap a ribbon carefully around each box and tie a bow, having filled the boxes with chocolates or sweets. Pack into gift boxes.

Fruit Fondant Chocolates

These chocolates are simple to make using pre-formed plastic moulds, yet look very professional. Fruit fondant is available from sugarcraft shops and comes in a variety of flavours including coffee and nut. Try a mixture of flavours using a small quantity of each, or use just a single flavour.

Makes 24

INGREDIENTS
225 g/8 oz/8 squares plain, milk or white chocolate
115 g/4 oz/1 cup real fruit liquid fondant
15–20 ml/3–4 tsp cooled boiled water

DECORATION
15 ml/1 tbsp melted plain, milk or white chocolate

milk chocolate

plain chocolate

white chocolate

1 Melt the chocolate. Use a piece of cotton wool to polish the insides of the chocolate moulds, ensuring that they are spotlessly clean. Fill up the shapes in one plastic tray to the top, leave for a few seconds, then invert the tray over the bowl of melted chocolate allowing the excess chocolate to fall back into the bowl. Sit the tray on the work surface and draw a palette knife across the top to remove the excess chocolate and to neaten the edges. Chill until set. Repeat to fill the remaining trays.

2 Sift the fruit fondant mixture into a bowl. Gradually stir in enough water to give it the consistency of thick cream. Place the fondant in a greaseproof paper piping bag, fold down the top and snip off the end. Fill each chocolate case almost to the top by piping in the fondant. Leave for 30 minutes or until a skin has formed on the surface of the fondant.

3 Spoon the remaining melted chocolate over the fondant to fill each mould level with the top. Chill until the chocolate has set hard. Invert the tray and press out the chocolates one by one. Place the melted chocolate of a contrasting colour into a greaseproof paper piping bag, fold down the top, snip off the point and pipe lines across the top of each chocolate. Allow to set, then pack into pretty boxes and tie with ribbon.

Chocolate Truffles

These are popular with almost everybody; simply use different combinations of chocolate and flavourings to make your favourites.

Makes 60

INGREDIENTS
115 g/4 oz/4 squares plain chocolate
115 g/4 oz/4 squares milk chocolate
175 g/6 oz/6 squares white chocolate
175 ml/6 fl oz/¾ cup double cream

FLAVOURINGS
30 ml/2 tbsp dark rum
30 ml/2 tbsp Tia Maria
30 ml/2 tbsp apricot brandy

COATINGS
45 g/3 tbsp coarsely grated plain chocolate
45 g/3 tbsp coarsely grated milk chocolate
45 g/3 tbsp coarsely grated white chocolate

milk chocolate

plain chocolate

white chocolate

1 Melt each type of chocolate in a separate bowl. Place the cream in a small saucepan and heat gently until hot but not boiling. Allow to cool. Stir ⅓ of the cream into each of the bowls and blend evenly. Add the rum to the plain chocolate and whisk until the mixture becomes lighter in colour. Whisk the Tia Maria into the milk chocolate and lastly whisk the apricot brandy into the white chocolate.

2 Allow the 3 mixtures to thicken, giving them an occasional stir, until they are thick enough to divide into equal spoonfuls. Line 3 baking sheets with non-stick baking paper. Place about 20 teaspoons of each flavoured chocolate mixture, well spaced apart, onto the 3 baking sheets and chill until firm enough to roll into small balls.

3 Place each of the grated chocolates into separate dishes. Shape the plain chocolate truffles into neat balls and roll in grated plain chocolate to coat evenly. Repeat with the milk chocolate truffles and grated milk chocolate and the white chocolate truffles and grated white chocolate. Chill the truffles until firm, then arrange neatly in boxes, bags or tins and tie with festive ribbon.

Chocolate Yule Log

This makes a delicious alternative to Christmas cake and is a real treat for chocolate lovers. Use the quantities below to make 4 individual logs if you are giving them as gifts.

*Makes 1 large or
4 small logs*

INGREDIENTS
3 eggs
75 g/3 oz/5 tbsp caster sugar, plus
  extra for sprinkling
65 g/2½ oz/¾ cup self-raising flour
15 g/½ oz/1 tbsp cocoa

CHOCOLATE CREAM
75 g/3 oz/5 tbsp caster sugar
75 ml/5 tbsp water
3 egg yolks
175 g/6 oz/¾ cup unsalted butter
75 g/3 oz/3 squares plain chocolate,
  melted

DECORATION
75 g/3 oz marzipan
green and red food colourings
icing sugar and cocoa, to dust

eggs

plain chocolate

*marzipan
decorations*

1 Preheat the oven to 190°C/375°F/ Gas 5. Lightly grease a 33 × 23 cm/13 × 9 in Swiss roll tin and line with non-stick baking paper. Place the eggs and sugar in a heatproof bowl over a saucepan of simmering water. Whisk the mixture until thick and pale, then remove the bowl from the saucepan. Continue to whisk until cool and thick, so that when the whisk is lifted it leaves a trail on the surface of the mixture.

2 Sift the flour and cocoa over the surface of the mixture and use a spatula to fold in carefully until all the flour has been incorporated. Pour the mixture into the tin, tilt to level the mixture and bake in the oven for 18–20 minutes or until the cake springs back when lightly pressed in the centre.

4 To make the chocolate cream, place the sugar and water into a saucepan. Heat gently until the sugar has dissolved, stirring occasionally. Boil rapidly to thread stage, 107°C/225°F on a sugar thermometer, or press a drop of syrup between 2 teaspoons; when pulled apart a thread should form. Place the egg yolks in a bowl; whisking well, gradually pour in the syrup. Whisk until the mixture is thick and pale. Leave to cool. Beat the butter until light and fluffy and gradually beat in the egg mixture until thick and fluffy. Fold in the melted chocolate.

3 Place a piece of non-stick baking paper onto a work surface and sprinkle with caster sugar. Invert the sponge onto the paper and carefully remove the lining paper. Using a sharp knife, trim off all the edges and loosely roll up the sponge cake, including the paper, into a neat roll. Start from the long edge if you are making individual rolls or the short edge if you are making one large roll.

5 Unroll the Swiss roll and remove the paper. Spread with half the chocolate cream and re-roll neatly. Spread the outside with the remaining chocolate cream and mark the surface with a palette knife to make it look like 'bark'. Chill to set the icing. Cut into 4 if making individual rolls.

6 Colour ⅓ of the marzipan green and a tiny piece bright red with the food colourings. Roll out the green marzipan thinly and cut out 12 leaves using a holly leaf cutter. Mould lots of tiny berries from the red marzipan and 6 tiny toadstools from the plain marzipan. Decorate the chocolate log or logs with holly leaves, berries and toadstools. Dust with icing sugar and cocoa.

Chocolate Christmas Cakes

This recipe may also be made as one 20 cm/8 in square cake but 4 individual cakes look even more tempting and may be packed into pretty boxes.

Makes 4

INGREDIENTS
275 g/10 oz/2½ cups self-raising flour
15 g/1 tbsp baking powder
50 g/2 oz/¼ cup cocoa
250 g/9 oz/1 cup 2 tbsp caster sugar
150 ml/¼ pint/⅔ cup sunflower oil
350 ml/12 fl oz/1½ cups water

ICING AND DECORATION
4 × 15 cm/6 in square silver cake
    boards
90 ml/6 tbsp Apricot Glaze (see
    Introduction)
1 kg/2¼ lb marzipan
900 g/2 lb chocolate sugarpaste
red, yellow and green food colourings
2 m/2 yd red ribbon
2 m/2 yd green ribbon

biscuit cutters

chocolate sugarpaste

marzipan

ribbon

1 Preheat the oven to 160°C/325°F/Gas 3. Grease a 20 cm/8 in square cake tin and line with greaseproof paper. Sift the flour, baking powder, cocoa and caster sugar into a mixing bowl.

2 Add the oil and water and mix together with a wooden spoon, beating until smooth and glossy. Pour into the prepared tin and bake in the oven for about 1 hour or until the cake springs back when pressed in the centre.

3 Cool the cake in the tin for 15 minutes, then turn out, remove the paper and invert on to a wire rack. When completely cold, cut into 4 equal pieces, place each on a separate cake board and brush with Apricot Glaze.

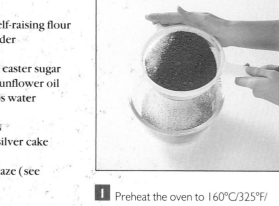

4 Divide the marzipan into 4 equal pieces and roll out a piece large enough to cover one cake. Place over the cake, press neatly into shape and trim off the excess marzipan at the base of the board. Knead the trimmings together and repeat to cover the remaining 3 cakes.

5 Divide the chocolate sugarpaste into 4 pieces and repeat the process, rolling out each piece thinly to cover each cake. Colour the remaining marzipan ⅓ red, ⅓ yellow and ⅓ green with the food colourings. Thinly roll out each piece and cut into 1 cm/½ in strips.

6 Lay alternate strips together and cut out 4 shapes using biscuit cutters. Arrange the shapes on top of each cake. Measure and fit the red and green ribbons around each cake and tie a bow. Pack into pretty boxes, tie with ribbons and label.

Festive Gingerbread

These brightly decorated gingerbread biscuits are fun to make and may be used as edible Christmas tree decorations.

Makes 20

INGREDIENTS
30 ml/2 tbsp golden syrup
15 ml/1 tbsp black treacle
50 g/2 oz/¼ cup light soft brown
    sugar
25 g/1 oz/2 tbsp butter
175 g/6 oz/1½ cups plain flour
¾ tsp bicarbonate of soda
½ tsp ground mixed spice
1½ tsp ground ginger
1 egg yolk

ICING AND DECORATION
½ quantity Royal Icing (see
    Introduction)
red, yellow and green food colourings
brightly coloured ribbons

biscuit cutters

ginge

egg

1 Preheat the oven to 190°C/375°F/ Gas 5. Line several baking sheets with non-stick baking paper. Place the syrup, treacle, sugar and butter into a saucepan. Heat gently, stirring occasionally, until the butter has melted.

2 Sift the flour, bicarbonate of soda, mixed spice and ginger into a bowl. Using a wooden spoon stir in the treacle mixture and the egg yolk and mix to a soft dough. Knead on a lightly floured surface until smooth.

3 Roll out the dough thinly and using a selection of festive cutters, stamp out as many shapes as possible, kneading and re-rolling the dough as necessary. Arrange the shapes well spaced apart on the baking sheets. Make a hole in the top of each shape using a drinking straw if you wish to use the biscuits as hanging decorations.

4 Bake in the oven for 15–20 minutes or until risen and golden and leave to cool on the baking sheets before transferring to a wire rack using a palette knife.

5 Divide the Royal Icing into 4 and colour ¼ red, ¼ yellow and ¼ green using the food colourings. Make 4 greaseproof paper piping bags and fill each one with the different coloured icings. Fold down the tops and snip off the points.

6 Pipe lines, dots, and zigzags on the gingerbread biscuits using the coloured icings. Leave to dry. Thread ribbons through the holes in the biscuits.

Hogmanay Shortbread

Light, crisp shortbread looks so professional when shaped in a mould, although you could also shape it by hand.

Makes 2 large or 8 individual shortbreads

INGREDIENTS
175 g/6 oz/¾ cup plain flour
50 g/2 oz/¼ cup cornflour
50 g/2 oz/¼ cup caster sugar
115 g/4 oz/½ cup unsalted butter

flour

sugar

butter

1 Preheat the oven to 160°C/325°F/Gas 3. Lightly flour the mould and line a baking sheet with non-stick baking paper. Sift the flour, cornflour and sugar into a mixing bowl. Cut the butter into pieces and rub into the flour mixture until it binds together and you can knead it into a soft dough.

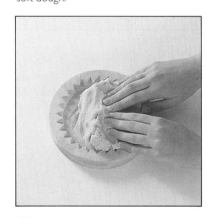

2 Place the dough into the mould and press to fit neatly. Invert the mould onto the baking sheet and tap firmly to release the dough shape. Bake in the oven for 35–40 minutes or until pale golden.

3 Sprinkle the top of the shortbread with a little caster sugar and cool on the baking sheet. Wrap in cellophane paper or place in a box tied with ribbon.

Christmas Tree Biscuits

These biscuits make an appealing gift. They look wonderful hung on a Christmas tree or in front of a window to catch the light.

Makes 12

INGREDIENTS
175 g/6 oz/1½ cups plain flour
75 g/3 oz/5 tbsp butter
40 g/1½ oz/3 tbsp caster sugar
1 egg white
30 ml/2 tbsp orange juice
225 g/8 oz coloured fruit sweets

DECORATION
coloured ribbons

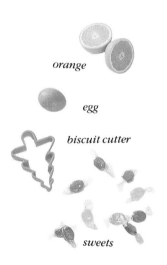

orange

egg

biscuit cutter

sweets

1 Preheat the oven to 180°C/350°F/ Gas 4. Line 2 baking sheets with non-stick baking paper. Sift the flour into a mixing bowl. Cut the butter into pieces and rub into the flour until the mixture resembles fine breadcrumbs. Stir in the sugar, egg white and enough orange juice to form a soft dough. Knead on a lightly floured surface until smooth.

2 Roll out thinly and stamp out as many shapes as possible using a Christmas tree cutter. Transfer the shapes to the lined baking sheets well spaced apart. Knead the trimmings together. Using a 1 cm/½ in round cutter or the end of a plain meringue piping nozzle, stamp out and remove 6 rounds from each tree shape. Cut each sweet into 3 and place a piece in each hole. Make a small hole at the top of each tree to thread through the ribbon.

3 Bake in the oven for 15–20 minutes, until the biscuits are slightly gold in colour and the sweets have melted and filled the holes. Cool on the baking sheets. Repeat until you have used up the remaining biscuit dough and sweets. Thread short lengths of ribbon through the holes so that you can hang up the biscuits.

Gingerbread House

This gingerbread house makes a memorable family gift, especially if filled with lots of little gifts and surprises.

Makes 1

INGREDIENTS
90 ml/6 tbsp golden syrup
30 ml/2 tbsp black treacle
75 g/3 oz/⅓ cup light soft brown
  sugar
75 g/3 oz/5 tbsp butter
450 g/1 lb/4 cups plain flour
15 g/1 tbsp ground ginger
15 g/1 tbsp bicarbonate of soda
2 egg yolks
225 g/8 oz barley sugar sweets

ICING AND DECORATION
1 quantity Royal Icing (see
  Introduction)
25 cm/10 in square silver cake board

black treacle

biscuit cutters

barley sugar sweets

eggs

golden syrup

1 Preheat the oven to 190°C/375°F/ Gas 5. Line several baking sheets with non-stick baking paper. Cut out the templates. Place the syrup, treacle, sugar and butter in a saucepan and heat gently, stirring occasionally until melted.

2 Sift the flour, ginger and bicarbonate of soda into a bowl. Add the egg yolks and pour in the treacle mixture, stirring with a wooden spoon to form a soft dough. Knead on a lightly floured surface until smooth and place in a polythene bag. Cut off ⅓ of the dough and roll out thinly.

3 Place the template for the end walls at one end and cut neatly around the shape using a sharp knife. Repeat to cut another end wall. Using a 2.5 cm/1 in round cutter, stamp out 1 round window on each end piece. Cut a door shape on each end piece using a 2.5 cm/1 in square cutter and rounding off the tops. Place a sweet in each opening and bake in the oven for 8–10 minutes until the sweet has filled the frame and the gingerbread is golden. Cool on the baking sheet.

4 Repeat the above instructions using the remaining dough for the 2 side walls and the two roof pieces. Using the 2.5 cm/1 in square cutter, stamp out 2 window shapes for each wall piece. Using the 2.5 cm/1 in round cutter, stamp out 3 round windows on each roof piece. Place sweets in the openings and bake as before.

5 Make the Royal Icing. Place some of the icing in a greaseproof paper piping bag fitted with a No. 2 plain writing nozzle. Pipe lines, loops and circles around the windows, doors and on the walls and roof to decorate. Pipe beads of icing in groups of 3 all over the remaining spaces and leave flat to dry.

TEMPLATES FOR THE GINGERBREAD HOUSE

1 For the side wall, measure and cut out a rectangle 15 cm × 10 cm (6 in × 4 in) from stiff card.

2 For the pitch of the roof, measure and cut out a rectangle 18 cm × 10 cm (7 in × 4 in). Measure 10 cm (4 in) up each long side and mark these points. Mark a centre point at the top of the short edge. Draw a line from each of the side points to the top point. Cut out.

3 For the roof, measure and cut out a rectangle 20 cm × 10 cm (8 in × 6 in) from stiff card.

6 To assemble the house, pipe a line of icing on the side edges of the walls and side pieces. Stick them together to form a box shape on the cake board. Pipe a line of icing following the pitch of the roof on both end pieces and along the top of the 2 roof pieces. Press gently in position and support the underneath of each roof while the icing sets. Pipe the finishing touches to the roof and base of the house. Dust the cake board with icing sugar to look like snow. Wrap ribbon around the edges of the board.

Cheeselets

These crispy cheese biscuits are irresistible, and will disappear in moments. Try using different cheeses sprinkled with a variety of seeds to give alternative flavours.

Makes about 80

INGREDIENTS
115 g/4 oz/1 cup plain flour
½ tsp salt
½ tsp cayenne pepper
½ tsp dry mustard
115 g/4 oz/½ cup butter
50 g/2 oz/½ cup grated Cheddar
50 g/2 oz/½ cup grated Gruyère
1 egg white, beaten
15 g/1 tbsp sesame seeds

sesame seeds

cayenne pepper

egg

Cheddar

Gruyère

dry mustard

1 Preheat the oven to 220°C/425°F/ Gas 7. Line several baking sheets with non-stick baking paper. Sift the flour, salt, cayenne pepper and mustard into a mixing bowl. Cut the butter into pieces and rub into the flour mixture until it begins to cling together.

2 Divide the mixture in half, add the Cheddar to 1 half and the Gruyère to the other. Using a fork, work each mixture into a soft dough and knead on a floured surface until smooth.

3 Roll out both pieces of dough very thinly and cut into 2.5 cm/1 in squares. Transfer to the lined baking sheets. Brush the squares with beaten egg white, sprinkle with sesame seeds and bake in the oven for 5–6 minutes or until slightly puffed up and pale gold in colour. Cool on the baking sheets, then carefully remove with a palette knife. Repeat the process until you have used up all the biscuit dough. Pack into tins or boxes and tie with ribbon.

Cocktail Biscuits

Tiny savoury biscuits are always a welcome treat. Try using different flavours and shapes and pack the biscuits into brightly coloured tins.

Makes about 80

INGREDIENTS
350 g/12 oz/3 cups plain flour
½ tsp salt
½ tsp black pepper
15 ml/1 tsp whole grain mustard
175 g/6 oz/¾ cup butter
115 g/4 oz/½ cup grated Cheddar
1 egg, beaten

FLAVOURINGS
5 g/1 tsp chopped nuts
10 g/2 tsp dill seeds
10 ml/2 tsp curry paste
10 ml/2 tsp chilli sauce

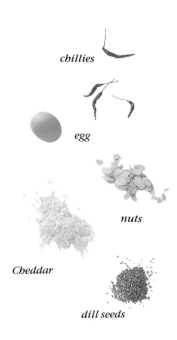

chillies

egg

nuts

Cheddar

dill seeds

1 Preheat the oven to 200°C/400°F/ Gas 6. Line several baking sheets with non-stick baking paper. Sift the flour into a mixing bowl and add the salt, pepper and mustard. Cut the butter into pieces and rub into the flour mixture until it resembles fine breadcrumbs. Use a fork to stir in the cheese and egg, and mix together to form a soft dough. Knead lightly on a floured surface and cut into 4 equal pieces.

2 Knead chopped nuts into one piece, dill seeds into another piece and curry paste and chilli sauce into each of the remaining pieces. Wrap each piece of flavoured dough in clear film and leave to chill in the fridge for at least an hour. Remove from the clear film and roll out one piece at a time.

3 Using a heart-shaped cutter, stamp out about 20 shapes from the curry-flavoured dough and use a club-shaped cutter to cut out the chilli-flavoured dough. Arrange the shapes well spaced apart on the baking sheets and bake in the oven for 6–8 minutes or until slightly puffed up and pale gold in colour. Cool on wire racks. Repeat with remaining flavoured dough using spade- and diamond-shaped cutters. Knead any trimmings together, re-roll and stamp out and bake as above.

Striped Biscuits

These biscuits may be made in different flavours and colours and look wonderful tied in bundles or packed into boxes. Eat them with ice cream or light desserts.

Makes 25

INGREDIENTS
25 g/1 oz/1 square white chocolate, melted
red and green food colouring dusts
2 egg whites
90 g/3½ oz/⅓ cup caster sugar
50 g/2 oz/½ cup plain flour
50 g/2 oz/4 tbsp unsalted butter, melted

egg

icing bag

white chocolate

1 Preheat the oven to 190°C/375°F/ Gas 5. Line 2 baking sheets with non-stick baking paper. Divide the melted chocolate in 2 and add a little food colouring dust to each half to colour the chocolate red and green. Using 2 greaseproof paper piping bags, fill with each colour chocolate and fold down the tops. Snip off the points.

2 Place the egg whites in a bowl and whisk until stiff. Add the sugar gradually, whisking well after each addition, to make a thick meringue. Add the flour and melted butter and whisk until smooth.

3 Drop 4 separate teaspoonsful of mixture onto the baking sheets and spread into thin rounds. Pipe lines or zigzags of green and red chocolate over each round. Bake in the oven for 3–4 minutes or until pale golden in colour. Loosen the rounds with a palette knife and return to the oven for a few seconds to soften. Have 2 or 3 lightly oiled wooden spoon handles at hand.

4 Taking one round biscuit out of the oven at a time, roll it around a spoon handle and leave for a few seconds to set. Repeat to shape the remaining biscuits.

5 When the biscuits are set, slip them off the spoon handles onto a wire rack. Repeat with the remaining mixture and the red and green chocolate until all the mixture has been used, baking only one sheet of biscuits at a time. If the biscuits are too hard to shape, simply return them to the oven for a few seconds to soften.

6 When the biscuits are cold, tie them together with coloured ribbon and pack into boxes, tins or glass jars.

CAKES AND PUDDINGS

Mini Iced Christmas Cakes

A personal Christmas cake makes an extra special gift. Try improvising with your own designs, decorations and colour schemes

Makes 1 large or 4 individual cakes

INGREDIENTS

350 g/12 oz/1½ cups mixed dried fruit

50 g/2 oz/¼ cup glacé cherries, sliced

50 g/2 oz/½ cup flaked almonds

grated rind of ½ lemon

15 ml/1 tbsp brandy

115 g/4 oz/1 cup plain flour

½ tsp ground mixed spice

25 g/1 oz/⅓ cup ground almonds

90 g/3½ oz/½ cup unsalted butter, softened

90 g/3½ oz/½ cup dark soft brown sugar

½ tbsp black treacle

2 eggs

ICING AND DECORATION

4 × 10 cm/4 in square cake boards

60 ml/4 tbsp Apricot Glaze (see Introduction)

675 g/1½ lb white marzipan

900 g/2 lb ready-to-roll icing

red and green food colourings

1 Prepare a 15 cm/6 in square cake tin. Place the mixed dried fruit, cherries, flaked almonds, lemon rind and brandy into a large mixing bowl. Stir until thoroughly blended, cover with clear film and leave for 1 hour or overnight.

2 Preheat the oven to 150°C/300°F/ Gas 2. Sift the flour and mixed spice into another bowl, add the ground almonds, butter, sugar, treacle and eggs. Mix together with a wooden spoon and beat for 2–3 minutes until smooth and glossy. Alternatively use a food mixer or processor for 1 minute. Fold the fruit into the cake mixture until evenly blended. Place the mixture in the prepared tin, level the top and make a slight depression in the centre.

3 Bake the cake in the centre of the oven for 2¼–2½ hours or until a skewer inserted into the centre of the cake comes out clean. Leave the cake to cool in the tin. Spoon over a little extra brandy if desired. Remove the cake from the tin and wrap in foil until required.

 lemon

glacé cherries

almonds

 marzipan

4 Remove the lining paper and cut the cake into 4 square pieces. Place each cake on a small cake board and brush evenly with Apricot Glaze. Cut the marzipan into 4 pieces and roll out a piece large enough to cover one cake. Place over the cake, smooth over the top and sides and trim off the excess marzipan at the base. Repeat to cover the remaining 3 cakes.

5 Cut the ready-to-roll icing into 5 pieces, roll 4 pieces out thinly to cover each cake, smoothing the tops and sides and trimming off the excess icing at the bases. Knead the trimmings together with the remaining piece of icing and cut into 2 pieces. Colour one piece red and the other piece green using the food colourings. Roll out ½ of the red icing into a 25 × 15 cm/10 × 6 in oblong.

6 Cut the icing into 5 mm/¼ in strips and place diagonally across the cake working from corner to corner. Trim the strips at the base of the cake. Brush the ends of the strips with a little water and press onto the cake. Make a few loops of icing and place on top of the cake. Repeat to decorate the remaining cakes with green and finally red and green strips of icing. Pack into boxes when dry.

Mini Black Buns

Black bun is a traditional Scottish recipe with a very rich fruit cake mixture cooked inside a bun dough. This variation uses marzipan in place of the dough.

Makes 4

INGREDIENTS
50 g/2 oz/4 tbsp butter, melted, plus
   extra for brushing
225 g/8 oz/1 cup mixed dried fruit
50 g/2 oz/¼ cup glacé cherries,
   chopped
50 g/2 oz/½ cup chopped almonds
10 g/2 tsp grated lemon rind
25 g/1 oz/2 tbsp caster sugar
15 ml/1 tbsp whisky
50 g/2 oz/½ cup plain flour
5 g/1 tsp ground mixed spice
1 egg, beaten

DECORATION
30 ml/2 tbsp Apricot Glaze (see
Introduction)
450 g/1 lb white marzipan
purple and green food colourings

marzipan

lemon

dried fruit

almonds

glacé cherries

1 Preheat the oven to 150°C/300°F/ Gas 2. Cut out 4 × 15 cm/6 in squares of greaseproof paper and 4 squares of foil. Place the greaseproof paper squares on top of the foil squares and brush with a little melted butter.

2 Place the dried fruit, cherries, almonds, lemon rind, sugar, whisky, sifted flour and mixed spice into a large mixing bowl. Using a wooden spoon, stir until well mixed. Add the melted butter and egg and beat together until well blended.

3 Divide the mixture between the 4 paper and foil squares, draw up the edges to the centre and twist to mould the mixture into rounds. Place on a baking sheet and bake in the oven for 45 minutes or until the mixture feels firm when touched. Remove the foil and bake for a further 15 minutes. Open the paper and cool on a wire rack.

4 Remove the paper and brush each cake with Apricot Glaze. Cut off ¼ of the marzipan for decoration and put to one side. Cut the remainder into 4 pieces.

5 Roll out each piece thinly and cover the cakes, tucking the joins underneath. Roll each cake in the palms of your hands to make them into round shapes. Prepare a hot grill and place the cakes on to a baking sheet lined with foil.

6 Grill the cakes until the marzipan is evenly browned. Leave until cold. Colour ½ of the remaining marzipan purple and ½ green with food colourings. Cut out 4 purple thistle shapes, green leaves and stems and arrange them on top of each cake, moistening with a little water to stick. Wrap in cellophane and place into small cake boxes.

Individual Dundee Cakes

Dundee cakes are traditionally topped with almonds but also look tempting covered with glacé fruits.

Makes 3

INGREDIENTS
225 g/8 oz/1 cup raisins
225 g/8 oz/1 cup currants
225 g/8 oz/1 cup sultanas
50 g/2 oz/¼ cup glacé cherries, sliced
115 g/4 oz/¾ cup mixed peel
grated rind of 1 orange
300 g/11 oz/2¾ cups plain flour
½ tsp baking powder
5 g/1 tsp ground mixed spice
225 g/8 oz/1 cup unsalted butter, softened
225 g/8 oz/1 cup caster sugar
5 eggs

TOPPING
50 g/2 oz/½ cup whole blanched almonds
50 g/2 oz/¼ cup glacé cherries, halved
50 g/2 oz/½ cup glacé fruits, sliced
45 ml/3 tbsp Apricot Glaze (see Introduction)

orange

glacé cherries

almonds

peel

egg

glacé fruits

1 Preheat the oven to 150°C/300°F/Gas 2. Prepare 3 × 15 cm/5 in round cake tins. Place all the fruit and the orange rind into a large mixing bowl. Mix together until evenly blended. In another bowl sift the flour, baking powder and mixed spice. Add the butter, sugar and eggs. Mix together with a wooden spoon and beat for 2–3 minutes until smooth and glossy. Alternatively use a food mixer or processor for 1 minute.

2 Add the mixed fruit to the cake mixture and fold in using a spatula until well blended. Divide the cake mixture between the 3 tins and level the tops. Arrange the almonds in circles over the top of one cake, the glacé cherries over the second cake and the mixed glacé fruits over the last one. Bake in the oven for approximately 2–2½ hours or until a skewer inserted into the centre of the cakes comes out clean.

3 Leave the cakes in their tins until completely cold. Turn out, remove the paper and brush the tops with Apricot Glaze. Leave to set, then wrap in cellophane paper or clear film and place in pretty boxes.

Spiced Christmas Cake

This light cake mixture is flavoured with spices and fruit. It can be served with a dusting of icing sugar and decorated with holly leaves.

Makes 1

INGREDIENTS

225 g/8 oz/1 cup butter, plus extra for greasing
15 g/1 tbsp fresh white breadcrumbs
225 g/8 oz/1 cup caster sugar
50 ml/2 fl oz/¼ cup water
3 eggs, separated
225 g/8 oz/2 cups self-raising flour
7.5 g/1½ tsp ground mixed spice
25 g/1 oz/2 tbsp chopped angelica
25 g/1 oz/2 tbsp mixed peel
50 g/2 oz/¼ cup glacé cherries, chopped
50 g/2 oz/½ cup walnuts, chopped
icing sugar, to dust

angelica

egg

glacé cherries

walnuts

peel

1 Preheat the oven to 180°C/350°F/Gas 4. Brush a 20 cm/8 in, 1.5 litre/2½ pint fluted ring mould with melted butter and coat with breadcrumbs, shaking out any excess.

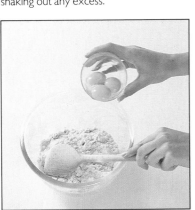

2 Place the butter, sugar and water into a saucepan. Heat gently, stirring occasionally, until melted. Boil for 3 minutes until syrupy, then allow to cool. Place the egg whites in a clean bowl, whisk until stiff. Sift the flour and spice into a bowl, add the angelica, mixed peel, cherries and walnuts and stir well to mix. Add the egg yolks.

3 Pour the cooled mixture into the bowl and beat together with a wooden spoon to form a soft batter. Gradually fold in the egg whites using a plastic spatula until the mixture is evenly blended. Pour into the prepared mould and bake for 50–60 minutes or until the cake springs back when pressed in the centre. Turn out and cool on a wire rack. Dust thickly with icing sugar and decorate with a sprig of holly.

Novelty Christmas Cakes

These individual cakes can be packed in their own little boxes to make unusual gifts for children.

Makes 2

INGREDIENTS
115 g/4 oz/1 cup self-raising flour
5 g/1 tsp baking powder
15 g/1 tbsp cocoa
115 g/4 oz/½ cup caster sugar
115 g/4 oz/½ cup soft margarine
2 eggs

DECORATION
45 ml/3 tbsp Apricot Glaze (see
    Introduction)
2 × 15 cm/6 in thin round cake
    boards
350 g/12 oz ready-to-roll icing
350 g/12 oz white marzipan
red, black, green, yellow and brown
    food colourings
white and red glitter flakes

marzipan

eggs

glitter flakes

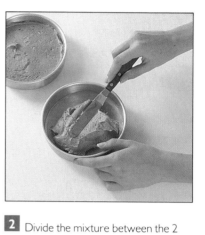

1 Preheat the oven to 160°C/325°F/ Gas 3. Grease and line the bases of 2 × 15 cm/6 in round sandwich tins. Place all the cake ingredients into a large mixing bowl. Mix together with a wooden spoon and beat for 2–3 minutes until smooth and glossy.

2 Divide the mixture between the 2 tins, smooth the tops and bake in the oven for 20–25 minutes or until the cakes spring back when pressed in the centre. Loosen the edges of the cakes and invert onto a wire rack. Remove the paper.

4 Colour ⅓ of the marzipan red and shape a mouth and nose; reserve the remainder. Colour a small piece of marzipan black and roll out thin lengths to outline the mouth and make the eyebrows and 2 crosses for the eyes.

Colour another small piece green for the ruffle. Colour another small piece yellow and grate coarsely to make the hair. Stick in position with Apricot Glaze and sprinkle with the white glitter flakes.

3 Brush both the cakes with Apricot Glaze and place on their cake boards. To make the clown cake, roll out ⅓ of the icing to a round large enough to cover one cake. Place the icing over the cake, smooth the surface and trim off the excess at the base. Mould 2 ears from the trimmings and press into position.

5 To make the Father Christmas cake, colour the remaining marzipan skin tone using a tiny amount of brown colouring and roll out thinly to cover ⅔ of the second cake. Trim to fit. Roll out ¾ of the red marzipan thinly and cover the remaining ⅓ of the cake to make the hat. Gather the excess together at one side for the hat. Mould a nose and mouth from the remaining red marzipan.

6 Coarsely grate the remaining white icing and use to trim the hat and to shape the beard, moustache and eyebrows. Gently press a small ball of grated white icing together to make a bobble for the hat. Shape 2 black eyes and press in position. Sprinkle red glitter flakes onto the hat to give a sparkle. Pack each cake into a small box with a lid and write a name tag.

Round Christmas Pudding

A round Christmas pudding makes a wonderful novelty gift. Special moulds are available from kitchen shops in large and small sizes.

Makes 1 large or
2 small puddings

INGREDIENTS
50 g/2 oz/4 tbsp butter, melted, plus
  extra for brushing
350 g/12 oz/1½ cups mixed dried
  fruit
200 g/7 oz/1 cup dried mixed fruit
  salad, chopped
50 g/2 oz/½ cup flaked almonds
1 small carrot, coarsely grated
1 small cooking apple, coarsely grated
grated rind and juice of 1 lemon
15 ml/1 tbsp black treacle
90 ml/3½ fl oz/6 tbsp stout
50 g/2 oz/1 cup fresh white
  breadcrumbs
50 g/2 oz/½ cup plain flour
5 g/1 tsp ground allspice
50 g/2 oz/¼ cup dark soft brown
  sugar
1 egg

apple

carrot

egg

lemon

dried fruit

almonds

1 Lightly butter 1 × 13 cm/5 in round Christmas pudding mould or 2 × 7.5 cm/ 3 in moulds, and place a disc of non-stick baking paper in the base of each half. Have a saucepan ready into which the pudding mould will fit comfortably.

4 Spoon the mixture into both halves of the mould so they are evenly filled. At this stage insert silver coins or miniature keepsakes wrapped several times in greaseproof paper.

2 Place all the dried fruits, nuts, carrot and apple into a large mixing bowl. Mix everything together with a wooden spoon. Stir in the lemon rind and juice, treacle and stout until well blended. Cover with clear film and leave in a cool place for a few hours or overnight.

5 Place the 2 halves of the mould together, stand on the base and clip firmly together to secure during cooking. Carefully place the mould into the saucepan. Half-fill the saucepan with boiling water, taking care that the water does not reach any higher than the join of the mould. Bring to the boil, cover and simmer very gently for 5–6 hours, being sure to replenish the saucepan with boiling water during the cooking time.

3 Add the breadcrumbs, sifted flour, allspice, sugar, butter and egg. Mix together until thoroughly blended.

6 Carefully remove half the mould and leave until the pudding is cold. Turn out, wrap in cellophane paper and tie with ribbon with a sprig of holly.

Flavoured Vinegars

Flavoured vinegars look extra special if you pour them into beautifully shaped bottles. Use fresh herbs and flowers, spices and soft fruits.

Makes 575 ml/1 pint/2½ cups of each flavour

INGREDIENTS
good quality red and white wine
    vinegar or cider vinegar

HERB VINEGAR
15 g/1 tbsp mixed peppercorns
2 lemon slices
4 garlic cloves
rosemary, thyme, tarragon and curry
    plant sprigs

SPICE VINEGAR
15 g/1 tbsp allspice berries
2 mace blades
10 g/2 tsp star anise
2 cinnamon sticks
1 orange

FRUIT VINEGAR
450 g/1 lb/3 cups raspberries
450 g/1 lb/3 cups gooseberries
450 g/1 lb/3 cups blackberries or
    elderberries

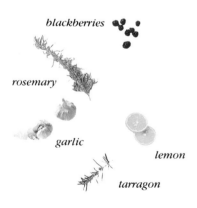

blackberries

rosemary

garlic

lemon

tarragon

1 Sterilize 2 bottles with corks or caps. To the first bottle add the peppercorns, lemon slices and garlic cloves. Place the herb sprigs together and trim the stems so they vary in length. Insert them into the bottle, placing the short ones in first.

4 Wash the raspberries, gooseberries and blackberries or elderberries separately and place into separate bowls. Crush with a wooden spoon.

2 Into the second bottle add the allspice berries, mace, star anise and cinnamon sticks. Cut 2 slices from the orange and insert into the bottle. Pare the rind from the remaining orange, taking care not to include any pith. Insert into the bottle.

3 Using white wine vinegar, fill the bottle containing the herbs up to the neck. Repeat to fill the bottle containing the spices with red wine vinegar. Cork or cap the bottles and store in a cool place.

5 Pour each fruit into a separate clean wide-necked jar and add 575 ml/1 pint/ 2½ cups of white wine vinegar. Cover and leave for 3–4 days in a cool place. Shake the jars occasionally to mix well.

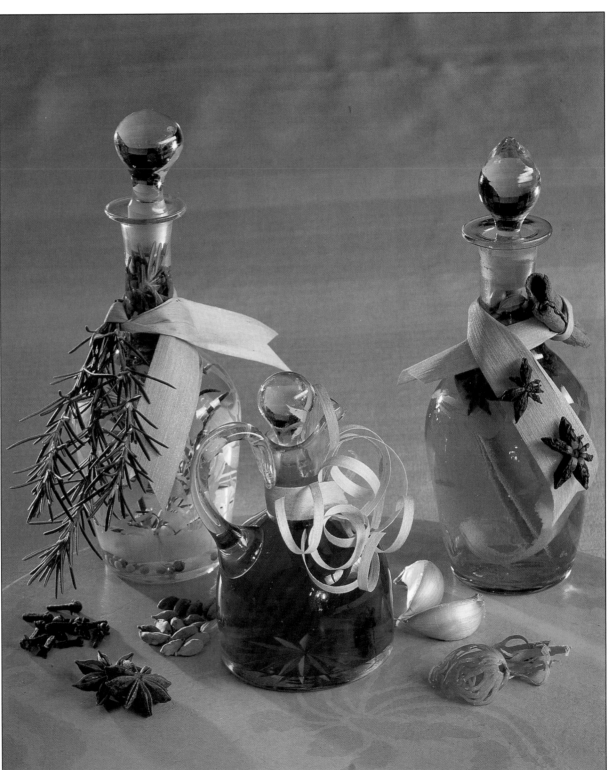

6 Strain each fruit separately through a jelly bag or a muslin-lined sieve into a stainless steel saucepan and boil for 10 minutes. Pour into sterilized bottles or jars and seal with lids or tops with plastic coated linings. Use all vinegars within 6 months.

Fresh Fruit Preserve

The wonderfully fresh flavour of this fruit spread makes it a welcome gift. To vary the recipe, use a mixture of soft fruits, or other individual fruits such as strawberries or blackberries.

Makes 900 g/2 lb

INGREDIENTS
675 g/1½ lb/3½ cups raspberries
900 g/2 lb/4 cups caster sugar
30 ml/2 tbsp lemon juice
100 ml/4 fl oz/½ cup liquid pectin

raspberries

lemon

1 Place the raspberries in a large bowl and lightly crush with a wooden spoon. Stir in the caster sugar. Leave for 1 hour at room temperature, giving the mixture an occasional stir to dissolve the sugar.

2 Sterilize several small jars or containers, and their lids if being used. Add the lemon juice and liquid pectin to the raspberries and stir until thoroughly blended.

3 Spoon the raspberry mixture into the jars, leaving a 1 cm/½ in space at the top if the preserve is to be frozen. Cover the surface of each preserve with a waxed paper disc and cover with a lid or cellophane paper and an elastic band. Don't use a screw-topped lid if the preserve is to be frozen. Allow to cool, then label and freeze for up to 6 months, or refrigerate for up to 4 weeks.

Flavoured Oils

Any good quality oils may be flavoured with herbs, spices, peppers, olives or anchovies. They look attractive in the kitchen, as well as being ready flavoured for use in cooking or salad dressings.

Makes 300 ml/¹/₂ pint/1¹/₄ cups of each flavour

INGREDIENTS
olive, grapeseed or almond oil

HERB OIL
sage, thyme, oregano, tarragon and
    rosemary sprigs
1 bay leaf sprig

SPICED OIL
30 g/2 tbsp whole cloves
3 mace blades
15 g/1 tbsp cardamom pods
15 g/1 tbsp coriander seeds
3 dried chillies
1 bay leaf sprig
2 lime slices
2 cinnamon sticks

MEDITERRANEAN OIL
2 mini red peppers
3 black olives
3 green olives
3 anchovy fillets
1 bay leaf sprig
strip of lemon rind

1 Have ready 3 bottles and corks which have been sterilized and are completely dry inside. Place all the fresh herb sprigs together and trim to fit inside the first bottle. Insert the short lengths first and arrange them using a long skewer, adding them stem by stem.

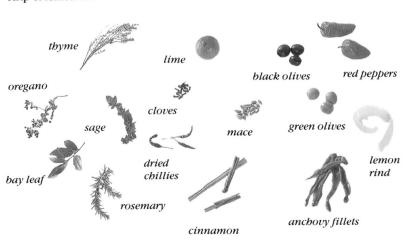

thyme

oregano

sage

bay leaf

lime

cloves

dried
chillies

rosemary

cinnamon

mace

black olives

green olives

anchovy fillets

red peppers

lemon
rind

2 Add the cloves, mace, cardamom pods, coriander seeds and chillies to the second bottle. Insert the sprig of bay leaves, lime slices and cinnamon sticks.

3 Grill the mini red peppers until they are tender, turning once. Add the olives, anchovies and peppers to the last bottle. Insert the bay leaf sprig and strip of lemon rind. Fill each bottle with the chosen oil and cork or cap. Label clearly and keep cool until required.

Red Pepper and Rosemary Jelly

This wonderful amber-coloured jelly may be made with either red or yellow peppers and flavoured with any full-flavoured herbs. It is delicious with cold meat, poultry, fish or cheeses.

Makes 1.75 kg/4 lb

INGREDIENTS
450 g/1 lb/8 tomatoes, chopped
4 red peppers, seeded and chopped
2 red chillies, seeded and chopped
rosemary sprigs
300 ml/½ pint/1¼ cups water
300 ml/½ pint/1¼ cups red wine
    vinegar
½ tsp salt
900 g/2 lb/5 cups jam sugar with
    added pectin
250 ml/8 fl oz/1 cup liquid pectin

peppers

rosemary

tomatoes

chillies

1 Place the tomatoes, peppers, chillies, a few rosemary sprigs and the water into a stainless steel saucepan and bring to the boil. Cover and simmer for 1 hour or until the peppers are tender and pulpy.

2 Suspend a jelly bag and place a bowl underneath. Sterilize the jelly bag by pouring through boiling water. Discard the water and replace the bowl.

3 Pour the contents of the saucepan slowly into the jelly bag. Allow the juices to drip through slowly for several hours but do not squeeze the bag or the jelly will become cloudy. Sterilize the jars and lids required.

4 Place the juice into a clean saucepan with the vinegar, salt and sugar. Discard the pulp in the jelly bag. Heat gently, stirring occasionally, until the sugar has dissolved. Boil rapidly for 3 minutes.

5 Remove the saucepan from the heat and stir in the liquid pectin. Skim the surface with a piece of kitchen paper to remove any foam.

6 Pour the liquid into the sterilized jars and add a sprig of rosemary to each jar. Place a waxed disc onto the surface of each and seal with a lid or cellophane paper and an elastic band. Allow to cool, then label and decorate with ribbons.

Crab Apple and Lavender Jelly

This fragrant, clear jelly looks even prettier with a sprig of fresh lavender suspended in the jar. Try using other fruits such as apples, quince or rosehips.

Makes about 900 g/2 lb

INGREDIENTS
900 g/2 lb/5 cups crab apples
1.75 litres/3 pints/7½ cups water
lavender stems
900 g/2 lb/4 cups granulated sugar

lavender

crab apples

2 Suspend a jelly bag and place a bowl underneath. Sterilize the jelly bag by pouring through some boiling water. Discard the water and replace the bowl.

3 Pour the contents of the saucepan slowly into the jelly bag. Allow the juice to drip slowly through for several hours but do not squeeze the bag or the jelly will become cloudy.

1 Cut the crab apples into chunks and place in a preserving pan with water and 2 stems of lavender. Bring to the boil and cover the pan with a piece of foil or a lid and simmer very gently for 1 hour, giving the mixture an occasional stir, until the fruit is pulpy.

4 Discard the pulp and measure the quantity of juice in the bowl. To each 575 ml/1 pint/2½ cups of juice add 450 g/ 1 lb/2 cups of sugar and pour into a clean pan. Sterilize the jars and lids required.

5 Heat the juice gently, stirring occasionally, until the sugar has dissolved. Bring to the boil and boil rapidly for about 8–10 minutes until setting point has been reached. When tested, the temperature should be 105°C/221°F. If you don't have a sugar thermometer, put a small amount of jelly on a cold plate and allow to cool. The surface should wrinkle when you push your finger through the jelly. If not yet set, continue to boil and then re-test.

6 Remove the pan from the heat and use a slotted spoon to remove any froth from the surface. Carefully pour the jelly into a jug, then fill the warm sterilized jars. Dip the lavender quickly into boiling water and insert a stem into each jar. Cover with a disc of waxed paper and with cellophane paper and a rubber band. Label when cold.

Peppers in Olive Oil

The wonderful flavour and colour of these peppers will add a Mediterranean theme to festive foods. Bottle the peppers separately or mix the colours together.

Makes enough to fill 3 × 450 g/1 lb jars

INGREDIENTS
3 red peppers
3 yellow peppers
3 green peppers
300 ml/½ pint/1¼ cups olive oil
½ tsp salt
½ tsp freshly ground black pepper
3 thyme sprigs

peppers

thyme

1 Prepare a hot grill or preheat the oven to 200°C/400°F/Gas 6. Put the whole peppers on a grill rack or onto a baking sheet. Place under the grill or in the oven and cook for about 10 minutes until the skins are charred and blistered all over. Turn frequently during cooking.

2 Allow the peppers to cool for at least 5 minutes, then peel off the skins. Remove the cores, seeds and stalks. Slice each of the peppers thinly, keeping each colour separate, and place each into a separate dish.

3 Pour ⅓ of the olive oil over each of the peppers. Sprinkle with salt and pepper and add a sprig of thyme to each dish. Stir to blend well. Sterilize 3 jars and lids and fill each with a mixture of peppers, or keep them separate. Top up each jar with the oil. Screw firmly down and label.

Christmas Chutney

This chutney makes the perfect accompaniment to cold meats, pâtés and cheese. It has a sweet but spicy flavour and the fruits may be changed for quince, greengage or rhubarb.

Makes 1.75 kg/4 lb

INGREDIENTS
450 g/1 lb/9 plums, stoned
450 g/1 lb/6 pears, peeled and cored
225 g/8 oz/2 cooking apples, peeled and cored
225 g/8 oz/4 sticks celery
450 g/1 lb onions, sliced
450 g/1 lb tomatoes, skinned
115 g/4 oz/½ cup raisins
15 g/1 tbsp grated fresh ginger root
30 ml/2 tbsp pickling spice
850 ml/1½ pints/3¾ cups cider vinegar
450 g/1 lb/2 cups granulated sugar

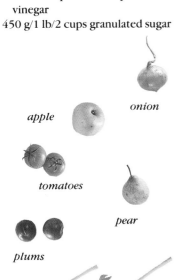

apple

onion

tomatoes

pear

plums

celery

ginger

1 Chop the plums, pears, apples, celery and onions and cut the tomatoes into quarters. Place all these ingredients with the raisins and ginger into a very large saucepan.

2 Place the pickling spice into a piece of muslin and tie with string to secure. Add to the saucepan with half the vinegar and bring to the boil, giving the mixture an occasional stir. Cook for about 2 hours.

3 Meanwhile sterilize the jars and lids. When all the ingredients are tender, stir in the remaining vinegar and the sugar. Boil until thick, remove the bag of spices and fill each jar with chutney. Cover with a wax paper disc and plastic lid and label when cold.

Fruits in Liqueurs

These eye-catching fruits in liqueurs are best made when the fruits are plentiful, cheap and in season. Choose from apricots, clementines, kumquats, physalis, cherries, raspberries, peaches, plums or seedless grapes and team them with rum, brandy, kirsch or Cointreau just to name a few.

Makes 450 g/1 lb

INGREDIENTS
450 g/1 lb/3 cups fresh fruit
225 g/8 oz/1 cup granulated sugar
150 ml/¼ pint/⅔ cup liqueur or
   spirits

apricots

clementines

kumquats

physalis

1 Wash the fruit, halve and stone apricots, plums or peaches. Peel back and remove the husk from physalis, hull strawberries or raspberries, and prick kumquats, cherries or grapes all over with a cocktail stick. Pare the rind from clementines using a sharp knife, taking care not to include any white pith.

2 Place 115 g/4 oz/½ cup of the sugar and 300 ml/½ pint/1¼ cups of water into a saucepan. Heat gently, stirring occasionally, until the sugar has dissolved. Bring to the boil.

3 Add the fruit to the syrup and simmer gently for 1–2 minutes until the fruit is just tender, but the skins are intact and the fruits are whole.

4 Carefully remove the fruit using a slotted spoon and arrange neatly into the warmed sterilized jars. Add the remaining sugar to the syrup in the pan and stir until dissolved.

5 Boil the syrup rapidly until it reaches 110°C/230°F or the thread stage. Test by pressing a small amount of syrup between 2 teaspoons; when they are pulled apart, a thread should form. Allow to cool.

6 Measure the cooled syrup, then add an equal quantity of liqueur or spirit. Mix until blended. Pour over the fruit in the jars until covered. Seal each jar with a screw or clip top, label and keep for up to 4 months.

Anchovy Spread

This delicious spread has a concentrated flavour and is best served with plain toast.

Makes 600 ml/1 pint/2¹/₂ cups

INGREDIENTS
2 × 50 g/2 oz cans anchovy fillets in
  olive oil
4 garlic cloves, crushed
2 egg yolks
30 ml/2 tbsp red wine vinegar
300 ml/¹/₂ pint/1 ¹/₄ cups olive oil
¹/₄ tsp freshly ground black pepper
30 g/2 tbsp chopped fresh basil or
  thyme

olive oil

red wine vinegar

eggs

basil

thyme

anchovy fillets

1 Drain the oil from the anchovies and reserve. Place the anchovies and garlic in a food processor. Process until smooth. Add the egg yolks and vinegar, and process until the egg and vinegar have been absorbed by the anchovies.

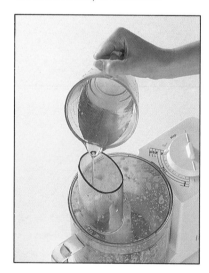

2 Measure out the oil into a measuring jug and add the reserved anchovy oil. Set the food processor to a low speed and add the oil drop by drop to the anchovy mixture until it is thick and smooth.

3 Add some freshly ground black pepper and fresh herbs, and blend until smooth. Spoon the mixture into small sterilized jars, cover and label. Store in the fridge.

Smoked Salmon Pâté

This luxury pâté makes a fine gift for a special person. Pack the pâté in a pretty dish to give as part of the gift. Store in the fridge.

Makes enough to fill 4 small ramekin dishes

INGREDIENTS

350 g/12 oz fresh salmon fillet
¼ tsp salt
½ tsp freshly ground black pepper
15 g/1 tbsp chopped fresh dill, plus sprigs to garnish
115 g/4 oz/4 slices smoked salmon
115 g/4 oz/½ cup curd or cream cheese
75 g/3 oz/5 tbsp unsalted butter
50 g/2 oz/1 cup fresh white breadcrumbs
5 ml/1 tsp lemon juice
30 ml/2 tbsp Madeira

lemon

dill

salmon fillet

smoked salmon

1 Preheat the oven to 190°C/375°F/ Gas 5. Put the salmon fillet on a large piece of greaseproof paper placed on top of a sheet of foil. Sprinkle with salt, pepper and dill. Seal the foil and place on a baking sheet. Cook in the oven for 10 minutes or until just tender. Leave until cold and remove the skin, saving any of the juices.

2 Cut out 4 pieces of smoked salmon to fit the bases of the 4 individual dishes. Cut out 4 strips to fit around the inside edges of each dish. Cover and chill.

3 Place the cooked salmon, its juices, the curd cheese, butter, breadcrumbs, lemon juice and Madeira into a food processor. Process until smooth. Divide the mixture between the dishes and press it down to fill each dish evenly. Cover the top with another piece of smoked salmon and decorate with a sprig of dill. Cover with clear film and chill.

Smokie Spread

This wonderful spread will be a welcome change of flavour at Christmas. Spread it on hot toast for an instant snack.

Makes enough to fill 4 small ramekin dishes

INGREDIENTS
115 g/4 oz/½ cup unsalted butter
350 g/12 oz smokie or kipper fillets, cooked
grated rind and juice of 1 lime
10 ml/2 tsp tomato purée
30 ml/2 tbsp whisky
50 g/2 oz/1 cup wholemeal breadcrumbs
½ tsp freshly ground black pepper

TO GARNISH
4 bay leaves
4 black olives, halved

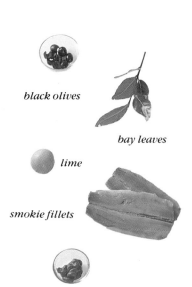

black olives

bay leaves

lime

smokie fillets

tomato purée

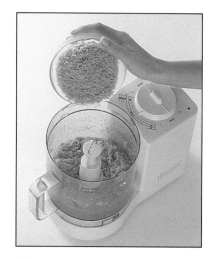

1 Melt 75 g/3 oz of the butter and place with the smokies into a food processor. Process until smooth. Add the lime rind and juice, tomato purée, whisky, breadcrumbs and pepper. Process again, until smooth.

2 Fill 4 individual ramekins with the smokie spread and press down well leaving a 1 cm/½ in space at the top. Cover and chill.

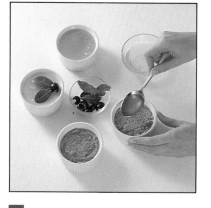

3 Melt the remaining butter and cool. Pour over each pot to fill to the top. Garnish with bay and olives. Chill until set, then cover with clear film.

Potted Cheese Rarebit

An instant 'cheese on toast' in a pot. Try using Gruyère cheese instead of the Cheddar as a variation. You may wish to serve it with a sprinkling of Worcestershire sauce or anchovy essence.

Makes 775 g/1¹/₂ lb

INGREDIENTS
50 g/2 oz/4 tbsp butter
15 ml/1 tbsp herbed French mustard
¹/₂ tsp freshly ground black pepper
100 ml/4 fl oz/¹/₂ cup ale or cider
450 g/1 lb mature Cheddar, grated

Cheddar

black pepper

French mustard

1 Place the butter, mustard, pepper and ale or cider into a saucepan. Heat gently, stirring occasionally, until boiling.

2 Add the cheese, take off the heat and stir until the cheese has melted and the mixture is creamy.

3 Pour the mixture into sterilized pots, cover and leave until cold. Chill to set, then label.

Farmhouse Pâté

This pâté is full of flavour and can be cut into slices for easy serving. You can make the pâté in 4 individual dishes, or make 1 pâté in a 450 g/1 lb container.

Makes 450 g/1 lb

INGREDIENTS
8 slices rindless streaky bacon
175 g/6 oz/2 chicken breasts
225 g/8 oz chicken livers
1 onion, chopped
1 garlic clove, crushed
½ tsp salt
½ tsp freshly ground black pepper
5 ml/1 tsp anchovy essence
5 g/1 tsp ground mace
15 g/1 tbsp chopped fresh oregano
75 g/3 oz/1 cup fresh white
  breadcrumbs
1 egg
30 ml/2 tbsp brandy
150 ml/¼ pt/⅔ cup chicken stock
10 ml/2 tsp gelatine

TO GARNISH
strips of pimento and black olives

onion

egg

chicken breast

chicken livers

streaky bacon

1 Preheat the oven to 160°C/325°F/ Gas 3. Press the bacon slices flat with a knife to stretch them. Line the base and sides of each dish with bacon and neatly trim the edges.

2 Place the chicken breasts and livers, onion and garlic into a food processor. Process until smooth. Add the salt, pepper, anchovy essence, mace, oregano, breadcrumbs, egg and brandy. Process until smooth.

3 Divide the mixture between the dishes and fill to the top. Cover each with double thickness foil and stand the dishes in a roasting tin. Add enough hot water to come halfway up the side of the dishes.

4 Bake in the centre of the oven for 1 hour or until firm to touch. Release the foil to allow the steam to escape. Place a weight on the top of each dish to flatten the surface until cool.

5 Pour the juices from each dish into a measuring jug and make up to 150 ml/ ¼ pint/⅔ cup with chicken stock. Heat in a small saucepan until boiling. Blend the gelatine with 2 tbsp water and pour into the hot stock, stir until dissolved. Allow to cool thoroughly.

6 When the pâté is cold, arrange strips of pimento and black olives on the top of each. Spoon the cold gelatine mixture over the top of each and chill until set. Cover each with clear film. Store in the fridge until required.

Savoury Butters

This selection of 8 tiny pots of unusual flavoured butters can be used as garnishes for meat, fish and vegetables, as a topping for canapés or as a tasty addition to sauces.

Makes about 50 g/2 oz/¹⁄₄ cup of each flavour

INGREDIENTS
450 g/1 lb/2 cups unsalted butter
25 g/1 oz/2 tbsp Stilton
3 anchovy fillets
5 ml/1 tsp curry paste
1 garlic clove, crushed
10 g/2 tsp finely chopped fresh
    tarragon
15 ml/1 tbsp creamed horseradish
15 g/1 tbsp chopped fresh parsley
5 g/1 tsp grated lime rind
¹⁄₄ tsp chilli sauce

Stilton

lime

tarragon

garlic

parsley

anchovy fillets

1 Place the butter in a food processor. Process until light and fluffy. Divide the butter into 8 portions.

2 Crumble the Stilton and mix together with a portion of butter. Pound the anchovies to a paste in a pestle and mortar and mix with the second portion of butter. Stir the curry paste into the third, and the crushed garlic into the fourth portion.

3 Stir the tarragon into the fifth portion and the creamed horseradish into the sixth portion. Into the seventh portion add the parsley and the lime rind, and to the last portion add the chilli sauce. Pack each flavoured butter into a tiny sterilized jar and label clearly. Store in the fridge.

Brandy Butter

No Christmas pudding is complete without brandy butter and it is simple to make. Pack into pretty jars or china containers tied with festive ribbon.

Makes 675 g/1¹/₂ lb

INGREDIENTS
225 g/8 oz/1 cup unsalted butter
225 g/8 oz/1 cup caster sugar
100 ml/4 fl oz/¹/₂ cup brandy

DECORATION
marzipan holly leaves and berries

brandy

caster sugar

marzipan decorations

butter

1 Bring the butter to room temperature before using, then place in a bowl or a food processor. Beat with a wooden spoon until light and smooth, or process until smooth.

2 Add the sugar and beat or process until the mixture is light and fluffy. Continue to beat or process adding the brandy a little at a time, beating or processing well after each addition. Do not add the brandy too quickly or the mixture will curdle.

3 Spoon the brandy butter into clean jars and seal with clean lids. Label and chill. Tie with pretty ribbon and a gift label. To decorate, pipe into small dishes using a fluted nozzle and decorate with small marzipan holly leaves and berries.

Christmas Cards

These decorative sugar greetings cards make ideal gifts. The Modelling Paste may be cut to any size and a variety of cutters or piping nozzles used to create the design. Double the quantity of Modelling Paste to make more cards.

Makes 4

INGREDIENTS
½ quantity Modelling Paste
old gold, green, red and purple food colourings
brown, red, green and purple food colouring pens
0.5 m/½ yd each of 2 mm/⅛ in wide brown, red, green and purple ribbon

food colouring pens

biscuit cutters

modelling paste

1 Make the Modelling Paste. Colour the paste a pale cream colour using a few drops of gold food colouring and cut into 4 pieces. Taking a piece at a time, roll out until the paste is 2 mm/⅛ in thick. Using a 9 cm/3½ in fluted oval cutter, stamp out 2 oval shapes. Stamp out a small oval from the centre of one shape using a 5 cm/2 in plain oval cutter.

2 Using a No. 1 plain writing nozzle, carefully stamp out tiny holes in each fluted shape around the edge of each oval. Make 2 holes 1 cm/½ in apart in the centre of the left-hand side on both shapes so they match together when the

ribbon is threaded through. Place the oval shape with the cut-out centre on a board. Using a small heart-shaped cutter, stamp out a series of hearts around the cut-out section. Use the plain nozzle to cut holes between the heart shapes.

MODELLING PASTE

INGREDIENTS
225 g/8 oz/1½ cups icing sugar
15 ml/1 tbsp gum tragacanth
5 ml/1 tsp liquid glucose
15–30 ml/1–2 tbsp water

1 Sift the icing sugar and gum tragacanth into a bowl. Make a well in the centre and add the liquid glucose and water. Mix together with your fingers to form a soft paste. Dust a surface with icing sugar and knead the sugar paste until smooth, white, pliable and free from cracks.

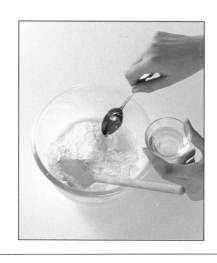

2 Place in a polythene bag or wrap in clear film and seal well to exclude all the air. Leave for 2 hours before use, then re-knead and use small pieces at a time, leaving the remaining Modelling Paste well sealed. Use a little white vegetable fat instead of icing sugar when kneading, rolling out or moulding the paste, to prevent it from becoming dry and brittle.

3 Leave the pieces to dry on a piece of foam sponge. Repeat to make 3 more cards in different shapes and sizes. When the cards are dry, arrange the 2 pieces of each card with the cut centres on top. Mark a series of dots within the cut-out centre, matching each food colouring pen to the ribbon colour, and write the name or greeting inside. Alternatively, cut out tiny holly leaves and berries and apply to the front of the card. Thread the ribbon through the holes to secure the cards together. They will keep indefinitely if stored in a cool, dry place.

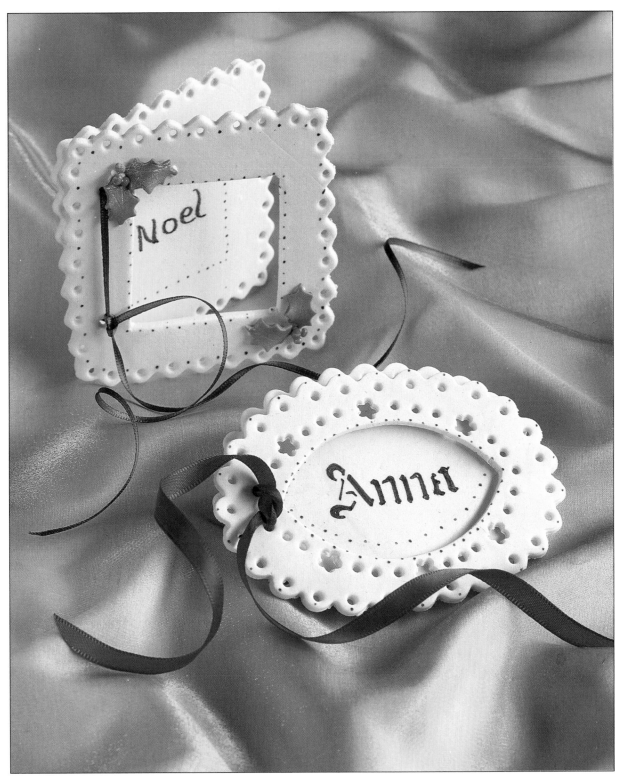

Sugar Boxes

These delightful boxes may be made in any size or shape you choose. Decorate them with a freehand design or apply cut out decorations if you prefer.

Makes 4

INGREDIENTS
1 quantity Modelling Paste
1 quantity Gum Glaze
green and red food colouring dusts or
ready-blended food colourings

cutter

paintbrushes

*food
colourings*

1 Measure around the outside of a plain round 7.5 cm/3 in cutter with a length of string and cut it to size. Dust the outside of the cutter with cornflour. Roll out a small piece of Modelling Paste thinly and cut to the length of the string and to the depth of the cutter. Gently ease the strip to fit inside the cutter so that the edges overlap, cutting away any excess paste. Brush the cut ends of the joins with a little Gum Glaze and press together to join neatly. Run a knife between the paste and the cutter to ensure the ring moves freely. Remove the cutter when the paste is firm.

2 Roll out another piece of paste thinly. Stamp out 2 rounds using the same cutter and place on a foam sponge. Mould a small knob for the lid, brush the underneath with Gum Glaze and press in position on the lid.

3 Brush the base edge of the box with Gum Glaze and place it in position on the round base. Repeat to make another 3 boxes. Leave all the pieces in a warm place to dry overnight. Using a fine pencil, draw a freehand design of holly leaves and berries, hearts, or your chosen design onto the side and lid of the box. Using food colouring dust mixed with a little Gum Glaze or ready-blended food colourings and a fine paintbrush, paint one colour at a time, cleaning the brush well before using each new colour. When dry, fill with small gifts or sweets.

GUM GLAZE

INGREDIENTS
15 ml/1 tbsp gum arabic
15 ml/1 tbsp water

1 Gum Glaze is much more effective than egg white for sticking together sugar paste items. It dries very quickly and sets the sugar paste. Blend the gum arabic with the water using a small whisk and beat until smooth and free from lumps. Place in a tiny screw-topped jar or container.

Napkin Rings

These pretty rings may be used as a table decoration and taken home afterwards as a keepsake.

Makes 4

INGREDIENTS
1 quantity Modelling Paste
red, green, gold and silver glitter food
   colouring dusts
30 g/2 tbsp Royal Icing (see
   Introduction)

biscuit cutter

Modelling Paste decorations

1 Make the Modelling Paste. Measure a piece of string to fit around the outside of a 7.5 cm/3 in plain cutter and cut to size.

2 Roll out a small piece of Modelling Paste to the length of the string and measuring 2.5 cm/1 in wide, and 3 mm/ 1/8 in thickness. Using a knife, cut out the measured shape and round off both ends.

3 Brush the surface of the Modelling Paste with red glitter dust to colour evenly. Place the strip of paste inside the cutter so the ends just meet. When the paste has set remove the cutter.

4 Colour the remaining strips green, silver and gold, and make another 3 napkin ring shapes. Place all 4 rings on a foam sponge and leave in a warm dry place for 48 hours until completely dry and hard.

5 To make the decorations, use some Modelling Paste to form a selection of tiny fruits and vine leaves following the instructions for Marzipan Fruits. Colour each fruit and leaf using the glitter dust and allow to dry. Using holly and ivy leaf cutters, make a selection of leaves and berries, rolling out the paste thinly and colouring with green and red glitter dusts. Mark the veins on the leaves with a knife and bend each leaf to dry over a wooden dowel or acrylic skewer.

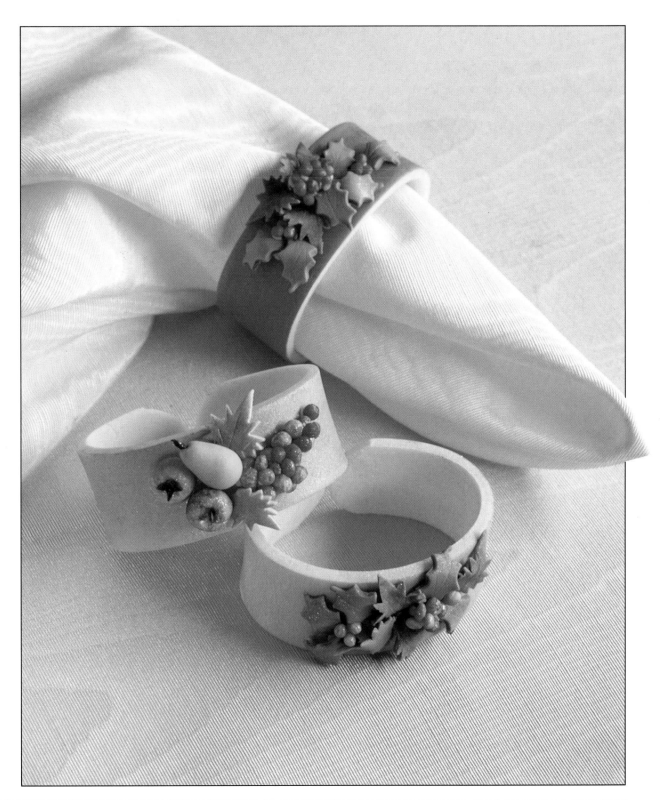

6 Apply the holly, ivy leaves and berries to the red and green napkin rings, securing each piece with a little Royal Icing. Arrange the fruit and vine leaves on the gold and silver napkin rings, securing them with Royal Icing. Leave overnight to dry and pack into individual boxes.

Hanging Christmas Decorations

Decorations made from sugar Modelling Paste dry as hard as ceramic tiles. Many shapes and designs may be accomplished by imagination and flair. Ready-to-roll icing may be used instead of Modelling Paste but allow much longer for drying.

Makes 6

INGREDIENTS
1 quantity Modelling Paste or 225 g/8 oz ready-to-roll icing or sugarpaste
1 quantity Gum Glaze
red and green food colourings
1.5 m/1½ yd red ribbon, 1 cm/½ in wide
3 m/3 yd green ribbon, 1 cm/½ in wide

Modelling Paste

biscuit cutters

ribbon

1 Make the Modelling Paste and Gum Glaze or use ready-to-roll icing or sugar-paste instead. Colour ⅓ of the paste a bright red and ⅔ a rich green using the red and green food colourings, and knead until evenly coloured and smooth. Keep in a polythene bag.

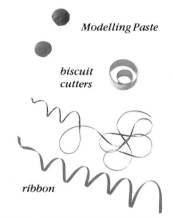

2 Using ½ of the green paste, roll out to a thickness of about 5 mm/¼ in. Using a 7.5 cm/3 in plain round pastry cutter, stamp out 3 rounds. Using a 5 cm/2 in plain cutter, stamp out the centre of each round to leave 3 rings. Take a small cocktail heart cutter and stamp out 3 heart shapes. Place all these cut-outs on a piece of foam sponge.

3 Brush the surface of one ring with Gum Glaze. Press some of the green paste through a garlic press, allowing the strands to fall evenly over the ring. Repeat to cover the remaining 2 rings. Roll out the red paste and using a 7.5 cm/3 in heart-shaped cutter, stamp out 3 hearts and secure the small hearts in the centre of each large heart using a little Gum Glaze. Make a hole in the top of each wreath and heart. Form lots of tiny berries and arrange at intervals on the wreath. Leave all pieces to dry hard, then thread ribbon through each.

Gold and Silver Christmas Bell Decorations

These are simply made by pressing sugar or Modelling Paste into a set of different sized bell-shaped moulds. They can be coloured, decorated or left plain.

Makes 6

INGREDIENTS
1 quantity Modelling Paste or
 225 g/8 oz ready-to-roll icing or
 sugarpaste
1 quantity Gum Glaze
cornflour, to dust
5 ml/1 tsp clear alcohol, gin or vodka
gold and silver food colouring dusts
1.5 m/1½ yd gold ribbon, 2 mm/⅛ in
 wide
1.5 m/1½ yd silver ribbon, 2 mm/⅛ in
 wide

bell moulds

food colouring dusts

ribbon

1 Make the Modelling Paste and Gum Glaze. Cut the paste into 6 even-sized pieces, returning 5 to the polythene bag. Lightly dust a work surface with cornflour and shake a little into the inside of the largest bell mould.

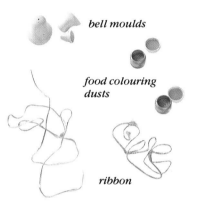

2 Gently ease the paste around the inside of a bell mould keeping the paste smooth. When the top end of the bell is smooth and a good shape, work down to the rim of the bell and trim off the excess with a knife. Pierce a hole in the top of the bell using a stainless steel needle. Repeat to make the medium- and small-sized bells, leave to dry. When the bells are hard, ease them out of the moulds and repeat to make another set.

3 Using a fine paintbrush brush the outside of one bell with alcohol. Dust with gold food colouring dust to coat evenly. Repeat to colour one set gold and one set silver. Cut each ribbon into 3 pieces. Mould 6 pea-shapes of paste for the 'clappers' and colour 3 gold and 3 silver. Make a hole in the centre of each, brush with Gum Glaze and insert the gold and silver ribbons. Thread the ribbon through each bell until the clapper is just above the rim. Press a small piece of paste, brushed with Gum Glaze, to the top of the bell to hold the ribbon in position, and tie the ribbon in a loop.

Candle Centrepiece

This arrangement of festive foliage and Christmas roses can be made in advance. Choose a brightly coloured candle for the centre.

Makes 1

INGREDIENTS
1 quantity Modelling Paste
1 quantity Gum Glaze
dark and light green and red food
   colourings
yellow and green food colouring dusts
30 g/2 tbsp Royal Icing (see
   Introduction)

Modelling Paste

food colourings

biscuit cutters

1 Make the Modelling Paste and Gum Glaze. Keep well sealed in a polythene bag during use. Divide the modelling paste into 3 pieces. Colour 1 piece dark green and 1 piece light green using the food colourings. Place in the polythene bag. Take a pea-sized piece from the remaining white paste and colour it bright red for the holly berries. Seal well.

2 To make the rose: roll out a small piece of white paste on an acrylic board so thinly that you can almost see through it. Using a Christmas rose cutter, cut out 5 petal shapes. Soften the edges by using a bone tool on a flower mat or piece of foam sponge and make them slightly cup-shaped. Roll out a tiny piece of dark green paste and cut out a calyx and place on the flower mat or foam.

3 Brush the calyx with a little Gum Glaze and arrange the petals on it one at a time so that they overlap slightly, and stick them together with Gum Glaze. Position the flower over the hole in the flower mat or pierced hole if you are using foam sponge. Mould a tiny piece of white paste into a bead shape, brush with Gum Glaze and dip into yellow dust to coat.

4 Place the yellow bead in the centre of the rose and place the rose over a round cutter to support the petals while drying. Leave to dry in a warm place and repeat to make another 4 roses.

5 Roll out the light green paste. Using large and small-sized holly cutters, stamp out 8 large and 8 small holly leaves. Mark in the veins with a knife and bend over an acrylic skewer or wooden dowel to give each leaf a realistic shape. Roll out the

dark green paste and cut out 8 medium-sized ivy leaves. Leave to dry. Mould lots of tiny red berries. Brush the surface of each leaf with Gum Glaze and green food colouring dust to give them a gloss.

6 Knead the remaining green coloured pastes together and roll into 2 × 25 cm/ 10 in pencil thin lengths. Twist together to form a rope and join the ends together to make a circle. Place on a board. Arrange the Christmas roses, holly and ivy leaves around the ring and add a few berries. Secure each element with a little Royal Icing. Leave to set hard in a warm place.

Marzipan Fruits

These eye-catching and realistic fruits will make a perfect gift for lovers of marzipan.

Makes 450 g/1 lb

INGREDIENTS
450 g/1 lb white marzipan
yellow, green, red, orange and
 burgundy food colouring dusts
30 g/2 tbsp whole cloves

marzipan

cloves

food colouring dusts

1 Cover a baking sheet with non-stick baking paper. Cut the marzipan into quarters. Take 1 piece and cut it into 10 even-sized pieces. Place a little of each of the food colouring dusts into a palette, or place small amounts spaced apart on a plate. Cut ⅔ of the cloves into 2 pieces, making a stem and core end.

4 Repeat as above using another piece of the marzipan to make 10 orange coloured balls. Roll each over the surface of a fine grater to give the texture of an orange skin. Press a clove core into the base of each.

2 Taking the 10 pieces, shape each one into a neat ball. Dip 1 ball into the yellow food colouring dust and roll between the palms of the hands to colour. Re-dip into the green colouring and re-roll to tint a greeny-yellow colour. Using your forefinger, roll one end of the ball to make a pear shape. Press a clove stem into the top and a core end into the base. Repeat with the remaining 9 balls of marzipan. Place on the baking sheet.

5 Take the remaining piece of marzipan, reserve a small piece, and mould the rest into lots of tiny marzipan beads. Colour them burgundy with the food colouring dust. Place a whole clove on the baking sheet. Arrange a cluster of burgundy beads in the shape of a bunch of grapes. Repeat with the remaining burgundy beads of marzipan to make another 3 bunches of grapes.

3 Cut another piece of the marzipan into 10 pieces and shape into balls. Dip each piece into green food colouring dust and roll in the palms to colour evenly. Add a spot of red colouring dust and roll to blend the colour. Using a ball tool or the end of a paintbrush, indent the top and base to make an apple shape. Insert a stem and core.

6 Roll out the remaining tiny piece of marzipan thinly and brush with green food colouring dust. Using a small vine leaf cutter, cut out 8 leaves, mark the veins with a knife and place 2 on each bunch of grapes, bending to give a realistic appearance. When all the marzipan fruits are dry, pack into gift boxes.

Turkish Delight

Turkish Delight is always a favourite at Christmas, and this versatile recipe can be made in minutes. Try different flavours such as lemon, crème de menthe and orange and vary the colours accordingly.

Makes 450 g/1 lb

INGREDIENTS
450 g/1 lb/2 cups granulated sugar
300 ml/½ pint/1¼ cups water
25 g/1 oz powdered gelatine
½ tsp tartaric acid
30 ml/2 tbsp rose-water
pink food colouring
25 g/1 oz/3 tbsp icing sugar, sifted
15 g/1 tbsp cornflour

tartaric acid

gelatine

rose-water

sugar

food colourings

1 Wet the insides of 2 × 18 cm/7 in shallow square tins with water. Place the sugar and all but 60 ml/4 tbsp of water into a heavy-based saucepan. Heat gently, stirring occasionally, until the sugar has dissolved.

2 Blend the gelatine and remaining water in a small bowl and place over a saucepan of hot water. Stir occasionally until dissolved. Bring the sugar syrup to the boil and boil steadily for about 8 minutes or until the syrup registers 127°C/260°F on a sugar thermometer. Stir the tartaric acid into the gelatine, then pour into the boiling syrup and stir until well blended. Remove from the heat.

3 Add the rose-water and a few drops of pink food colouring to tint the mixture pale pink. Pour the mixture into the tins and allow to set for several hours or overnight. Dust a sheet of greaseproof paper with some of the icing sugar and cornflour. Dip the base of the tin in hot water. Invert onto the paper. Cut into 2.5 cm/1 in squares using an oiled knife. Toss in icing sugar to coat evenly.

Orange, Mint and Coffee Meringues

These tiny, crisp meringues are flavoured with orange, coffee and mint chocolate sticks and liqueurs. Pile into dry, air-tight glass jars or decorative tins.

Makes 90

INGREDIENTS
25 g/1 oz/8 chocolate mint sticks
25 g/1 oz/8 chocolate orange sticks
25 g/1 oz/8 chocolate coffee sticks
½ tsp crème de menthe
½ tsp orange curaçao or Cointreau
½ tsp Tia Maria
3 egg whites
175 g/6 oz/¾ cup caster sugar
5 g/1 tsp cocoa

Tia Maria

eggs

crème de menthe

*chocolate
mint sticks*

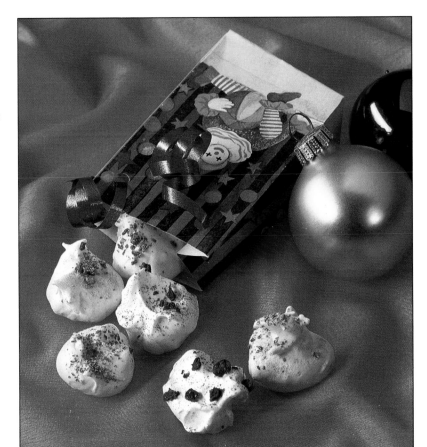

1 Preheat the oven to 110°C/225°F/ Gas ¼. Line 2–3 baking sheets with non-stick baking paper. Chop each flavour of chocolate stick separately and place each into separate bowls, retaining a teaspoonful of each flavour stick. Stir in the liquid flavourings to match the chocolate sticks.

2 Place the egg whites in a clean bowl and whisk until stiff. Gradually add the sugar, whisking well after each addition until thick. Add ⅓ of the meringue to each bowl and fold in gently using a clean spatula until evenly blended.

3 Place about 30 teaspoons of each mixture onto the baking sheets, well spaced apart. Sprinkle the top of each meringue with the reserved chopped chocolate sticks, matching the flavours. Bake in the oven for 1 hour or until crisp. Allow to cool and dust lightly with cocoa.

Creamy Fudge

A good selection of fudge always makes a welcome change from chocolates. Mix and match the flavours to make a gift-wrapped assortment.

Makes 900 g/2 lb

INGREDIENTS

50 g/2 oz/4 tbsp unsalted butter, plus extra for greasing
450 g/1 lb/2 cups granulated sugar
300 ml/½ pint/1¼ cups double cream
150 ml/¼ pint/⅔ cup milk
45 ml/3 tbsp water (this can be replaced with orange, apricot or cherry brandy, or strong coffee)

FLAVOURINGS

225 g/8 oz/1 cup plain or milk chocolate dots
115 g/4 oz/1 cup chopped almonds, hazelnuts, walnuts or brazil nuts
115 g/4 oz/½ cup chopped glacé cherries, dates or dried apricots

walnuts

almonds

glacé cherries

hazelnuts

plain chocolate dots

1 Butter a 20 cm/8 in shallow square tin. Place the sugar, cream, butter, milk and water or other flavouring into a large heavy-based saucepan. Heat very gently, stirring occasionally using a long-handled wooden spoon, until all the sugar has completely dissolved.

2 Bring the mixture to the boil and boil steadily, stirring only occasionally to prevent the mixture from burning over the base of the saucepan. Boil until the fudge reaches just under soft ball stage, 113°C/230°F for a soft fudge.

3 If you are making chocolate flavoured fudge, add the chocolate at this stage. Remove the saucepan from the heat and beat thoroughly until the mixture starts to thicken and become opaque.

4 Just before this consistency has been reached, add chopped nuts for a nutty fudge, or glacé cherries or dried fruit for a fruit-flavoured fudge. Beat well until evenly blended.

5 Pour the fudge into the prepared tin, taking care as the mixture is exceedingly hot. Leave the mixture until cool and almost set. Using a sharp knife, mark the fudge into small squares and leave in the tin until quite firm.

6 Turn the fudge out onto a board and invert. Using a long-bladed knife, cut into neat squares. You can dust some with icing sugar and drizzle others with melted chocolate if desired.

Macaroons

These little macaroons can be served as petit-fours or with coffee. To make chocolate macaroons, replace the cornflour with cocoa.

Makes 30

INGREDIENTS
50 g/2 oz/⅔ cup ground almonds
50 g/2 oz/¼ cup caster sugar
15 g/1 tbsp cornflour
¼–½ tsp almond essence
1 egg white, whisked
15 flaked almonds
4 glacé cherries, quartered
icing sugar or cocoa, to dust

egg

glacé cherries

almonds

1 Preheat the oven to 160°C/325°F/ Gas 3. Line 2 baking sheets with non-stick baking paper. Place the ground almonds, sugar, cornflour and almond essence into a bowl and mix together well using a wooden spoon.

2 Stir in enough egg white to form a soft piping consistency. Place the mixture into a nylon piping bag fitted with a 1 cm/ ½ in plain piping nozzle.

3 Pipe about 15 rounds of mixture on-to each baking sheet well spaced apart. Press a flaked almond onto half the macaroons and quartered glacé cherries onto the remainder. Bake in the oven for 10–15 minutes until firm to touch. Cool on the paper and dust with icing sugar or cocoa before removing from the paper.

Truffle Christmas Puddings

Truffles disguised as Christmas puddings are great fun to make and receive. Make any flavoured truffle, and decorate them as you like.

Makes 20

INGREDIENTS
20 plain chocolate truffles
15 g/1 tbsp cocoa
15 g/1 tbsp icing sugar
225 g/8 oz/1 cup white chocolate
   dots, melted
50 g/2 oz white marzipan
green and red food colourings
yellow food colouring dust

marzipan

chocolate truffles

food colouring dust

white chocolate dots

1 Make the truffles following the recipe on page 25. Sift the cocoa and icing sugar together and coat the truffles.

2 Spread ⅔ of the melted white chocolate over a piece of non-stick baking paper. Pick up the corners and shake to level the surface. Using a 2.5 cm/1 in daisy cutter, stamp out 20 rounds when the chocolate has just set. Place a truffle on the centre of each daisy shape, secured with a little of the reserved melted chocolate. Leave to set.

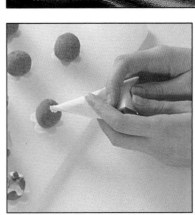

3 Colour ⅔ of the marzipan green and ⅓ red using the food colourings. Roll out the green thinly and stamp out 40 leaves using a tiny holly leaf cutter. Mark the veins with a knife. Mould lots of tiny red beads. Colour the remaining white chocolate with yellow food colouring dust and place in a greaseproof paper piping bag. Fold down the top, cut off the point and pipe over the top of each truffle to resemble custard. Arrange the holly leaves and berries on the top. When set, arrange in gift boxes and tie with ribbon.

Marshmallows

These light and fragrant mouthfuls of pale pink mousse are flavoured with rose-water. Try using orange-flower water as a contrast, and colour the sweets with a hint of orange food colouring.

Makes 500 g/1¼ lb

INGREDIENTS
oil, for greasing
45 g/3 tbsp icing sugar
45 g/3 tbsp cornflour
50 ml/2 fl oz/¼ cup cold water
45 ml/3 tbsp rose-water
25 g/1 oz powdered gelatine
pink food colouring
450 g/1 lb/2 cups granulated sugar
30 ml/2 level tbsp liquid glucose
250 ml/8 fl oz/1 cup boiling water
2 egg whites

egg

gelatine

icing sugar

rose-water

food colouring

1 Lightly oil a 28 × 18 cm/11 × 7 in Swiss roll tin. Sift together the icing sugar and cornflour and use some of this mixture to coat the inside of the tin evenly. Shake out the excess.

2 Mix together the cold water, rose-water, gelatine and a drop of pink food colouring in a small bowl. Place over a saucepan of hot water and stir occasionally until the gelatine has dissolved.

3 Place the sugar, liquid glucose and boiling water in a heavy-based saucepan. Stir over a low heat to dissolve the sugar completely. Ensure that there are no sugar crystals around the water line; if so, wash these down with a brush dipped in cold water.

4 Bring the syrup to the boil and boil steadily without stirring until the temperature reaches 127°C/260°F on a sugar thermometer. Remove from the heat and stir in the gelatine mixture.

5 While the syrup is boiling, whisk the egg whites stiffly in a large bowl using an electric hand whisk. Pour a steady stream of syrup onto the egg whites while whisking continuously for about 3 minutes or until the mixture is thick and foamy. At this stage add more food colouring if the mixture looks too pale.

6 Pour the mixture into the prepared tin and allow to set for about 4 hours or overnight. Sift some of the remaining icing sugar mixture over the surface of the marshmallow and the rest over a board or baking sheet. Ease the mixture away from the tin using an oiled palette knife and invert onto the board. Cut into 2.5 cm/1 in squares, coating the cut sides with the icing sugar mixture. Pack into glass containers or tins and seal well.

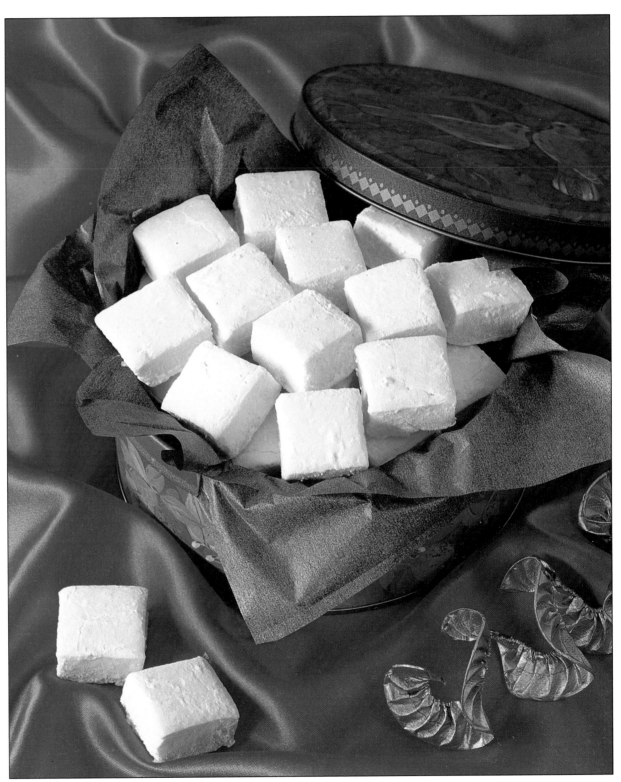

Glacé Fruits

These luxury sweetmeats are very popular at Christmas and they cost a fraction of the shop price if made at home. The whole process takes about 4 weeks, but the result is well worth the effort. Choose one type of fruit, or select a variety of fruits such as cherries, plums, peaches, apricots, starfruit, pineapple, apples, oranges, lemons, limes and clementines.

Makes 24 pieces

INGREDIENTS
450 g/1 lb fruit
1 kg/2¼ lb/4½ cups granulated sugar
115 g/4 oz/1 cup powdered glucose

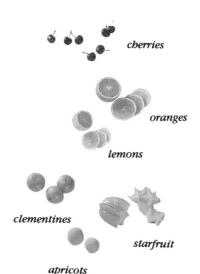

cherries

oranges

lemons

clementines

starfruit

apricots

1 Remove the stones from cherries, plums, peaches and apricots. Peel and core pineapple and cut into cubes or rings. Peel, core and quarter apples and thinly slice citrus fruits. Prick the skins of cherries with a stainless steel needle so the syrup can penetrate the skin.

2 Place enough of the prepared fruit in a saucepan to cover the base, keeping individual fruit types together. Add enough water to cover the fruit and simmer very gently, to avoid breaking it, until almost tender. Use a slotted spoon to lift the fruit and place in a shallow dish, removing any skins if necessary. Repeat as above until all the fruit has been cooked.

3 Measure 300 ml/½ pint/1¼ cups of the liquid, or make up this quantity with water if necessary. Pour into the saucepan and add 50 g/2 oz/4 tbsp sugar and the glucose. Heat gently, stirring occasionally, until dissolved. Bring to the boil and pour over the fruit in the dish, completely immersing it, and leave overnight.

4 DAY 2. Drain the syrup from the fruit into the saucepan and add 50 g/2 oz/ 4 tbsp sugar. Heat gently to dissolve the syrup and bring to the boil. Pour over the fruit and leave overnight. Repeat this process each day, draining off the syrup, dissolving 50 g/2 oz/4 tbsp sugar, boiling the syrup and immersing the fruit and leaving overnight on Days 3, 4, 5, 6 and 7.

5 DAY 8. Drain the fruit, dissolve 75 g/ 3 oz/½ cup sugar in the syrup and bring to the boil. Add the fruit and cook gently for 3 minutes. Return to the dish and leave for 2 days. DAY 10. Repeat as above for Day 8; at this stage the syrup should look like clear honey. Leave in the dish for at least a further 10 days, or up to 3 weeks.

6 Place a wire rack over a tray and remove each piece of fruit with a slotted spoon. Arrange on the rack. Dry the fruit in a warm dry place or in the oven at the lowest setting until the surface no longer feels sticky. To coat in sugar, spear each piece of fruit and plunge into boiling water, then roll in granulated sugar. To dip into syrup, place the remaining sugar and 175 ml/6 fl oz/¾ cup of water in a saucepan. Heat gently until the sugar has dissolved, then boil for 1 minute. Dip each piece of fruit into boiling water, then quickly into the syrup. Place on the wire rack and leave in a warm place until dry. Place the fruits in paper sweet cases and pack into boxes.

Rosehip Cordial

If you get the chance to collect rosehips from the hedgerows, this cordial makes a wonderfully Christmassy drink. If you can't find rosehips, replace them with blackcurrants.

Makes 1.75 litres/3 pints/7½ cups

INGREDIENTS
2.65 litres/4½ pints/11¼ cups water
1 kg/2 lb/6 cups rosehips
450 g/1 lb/4 cups granulated sugar

rosehips

COOK'S TIP

To sterilize, dissolve one crushed Campden tablet in 15 ml/1 tbsp of boiled water and add to each 600 ml/1 pint/2½ cups of cordial. Pour the cordial into the sterilized bottles and seal with a cork or stopper. Store the cordial in the fridge.

1 Sterilize 4 small bottles. Place 1.75 litres/3 pints/7½ cups of water in a large heavy-based saucepan and bring to the boil. Put the rosehips in a food processor and process until finely chopped. Add to the boiling water, bring back to the boil, cover with a lid and turn off the heat. Leave to infuse for 15 minutes.

2 Suspend a jelly bag and place a bowl underneath. Sterilize the jelly bag by pouring boiling water through the bag, then discard the water and replace the bowl. Strain the rosehips through the jelly bag and leave until the pulp is almost dry.

3 Return the pulp to the saucepan with another 900 ml/1½ pints/3¾ cups of water, bring to the boil, cover and infuse for 10 minutes as above and strain, mixing the 2 juices together. Pour the juices back into a clean saucepan and boil to reduce the mixture by half, to about 1 litre/1¾ pints/4 cups. Stir in the sugar, heat gently until dissolved, then boil for 5 minutes. Sterilize the cordial if it is going to be kept for longer than 4 weeks.

Christmas Spirit

This colourful drink has a sharp but sweet taste. It is excellent served as a winter warmer or after a meal, but it is also good as a summer drink with crushed ice.

Makes 700 ml/1¼ pints/3 cups

INGREDIENTS
450 g/1 lb/2 cups cranberries
2 clementines
450 g/1 lb/2 cups granulated sugar
1 cinnamon stick
500 ml/16 fl oz/2 cups vodka

cranberries

clementines

cinnamon sticks

1 Sterilize a large jar and lid. Place the cranberries in a food processor or use a pestle and mortar to crush them evenly. Spoon the cranberries into the jar. Pare the rind thinly from the clementines taking care not to include the white pith. Squeeze the juice and add with the rind to the jar.

2 Add the sugar, cinnamon stick and vodka to the jar and seal with the lid or a double thickness of plastic, and tie down securely. Shake the jar well to combine all the ingredients.

3 Store in a cool place for 1 month, shaking the jar daily for 2 weeks, then occasionally. When the drink has matured, sterilize some small pretty bottles and using a funnel with a filter paper inside, strain the liquid into the bottles and cork immediately. Label clearly and tie a gift tag around the neck.

Festive Liqueurs

These are easier to make than wines and may be made with a variety of flavours and spirits. All these liqueurs should be allowed to mature for 3 months before drinking.

Makes 850 ml/1½ pints/ 3¾ cups of each liqueur

PLUM BRANDY
450 g/1 lb plums
225 g/8 oz/1 cup demerara sugar
575 ml/1 pint/2½ cups brandy

FRUIT GIN
450 g/1 lb/3 cups raspberries,
   blackcurrants or sloes
350 g/12 oz/1½ cups granulated sugar
700 ml/1¼ pints/3 cups gin

CITRUS WHISKY
1 large orange
1 small lemon
1 lime
225 g/8 oz/1 cup granulated sugar
575 ml/1 pint/2½ cups whisky

orange

peaches

lemon

lime

blackcurrants

1 Sterilize 3 jars and lids. Wash and halve the plums, remove the stones and finely slice. Place the plums in the sterilized jar with the sugar and brandy. Crack 3 stones, remove the kernels and chop. Add to the jar and stir until well blended.

2 Place the raspberries, blackcurrants or sloes into the prepared jar. If using sloes, prick the surface of the berries using a stainless steel pin to extract the flavour. Add the sugar and gin and stir until well blended.

3 To make the Citrus Whisky, first scrub the fruit. Using a sharp knife or potato peeler pare the rind from the fruit, taking care not to include the white pith. Squeeze out all the juice and place in the jar with the fruit rinds. Add the sugar and whisky, stir until well blended.

4 Cover the jars with lids or double thickness plastic tied well down. Store the jars in a cool place for 3 months.

5 Shake the Fruit Gin every day for 1 month, and then occasionally. Shake the Plum Brandy and Citrus Whisky every day for 2 weeks, then occasionally. Sterilize the chosen bottles and corks or stoppers for each liqueur.

6 When each liqueur is ready to be bottled, strain, then pour into the bottles through a funnel fitted with a filter paper. Fit the corks or stoppers and label with a festive label.

INDEX

USEFUL ADDRESSES

Most of the equipment used in this book is available from good kitchen suppliers or large department stores. For more specialized equipment, consult the business directory for addresses in your area. The following companies provide a mail order service.

Beverly Dutton
c/o Squire's Kitchen
3 Waverly Lane
Farnham, Surrey
GU9 8BB
tel: 0252 711 749
(Sugarcraft specialist.
Catalogue available)

Lakeland Plastics Limited
Alexandra Building
Windermere, Cumbria
LA23 1BQ
tel: 05394 88100
(Catalogue available)